What the Bible Is All About for Moms

At last! A book that captures the immeasurable significance of a mother through the truths of God's Word. Never before have I felt my heart leap for joy while reading a devotional. Kathy's writings challenges the intellectual, calms the frazzled, and motivates the willing! I simply cannot wait to experience more!

ERIN CAMPBELL
Director/Executive Producer, Water Through the Word Broadcasting Productions

Kathy Pride is a resounding new voice who cuts to the heart of the spiritual matter, clarifying sometimes obscure Bible characters and wringing every drop of truth from God's Word with fresh insight. She truly does "Lighten the Mother Load" with pithy takeaways that leave you encouraged and empowered to apply scriptural principles to everyday life.

DEBORA M .COTY
Author of *Mom Needs Chocolate* and *Everyday Hope*

This book is a must-have for moms. In quick, easy-to-read chapters, Kathy Pride breaks down the entire Bible to show us what's in it and how it applies to our daily life as moms. Not only will I use this book for my own quiet times, but it is also a great resource to help answer my kids' questions about the Bible as well.

JILL HART
Founder of Christian Work At Home Moms (CWAHM.com)
Co-author of *So You Want to Be a Work at Home Mom*

With wit, honesty and truth, *What the Bible Is All About for Moms* reminds mothers of the dreams and promises that God has for their lives. It offers much biblical insight that all moms can apply to their lives. Kathy's wisdom will be great inspiration and encouragement for both stay-at-home moms and working mothers.

JESSICA TURNER
Founder of TheMomCreative.com

What an impressive and heartwarming book. As Moses was impacted by his mother, we too are profoundly influenced by moms who care and nurture so that their prayers and words of life from Scripture can create the potential miracle of Gods design. I enjoyed the words of insight that Kathy Pride wove into the fabric of this outstanding book of purpose, hope and encouragement. You too are called to make a difference in the life of an innocent and needy child.

LOREN MILLER, DPM
Executive Director, New Horizons Ministries (www.newhorizonsministries.net)

In this outstanding devotional, Kathy Pride admits, "I never set out to be a writer . . . but God had other plans for me. . . ." Those plans were apparently for her to breathe new life into the classic *What the Bible is All About* by Dr. Henrietta Mears. Kathy affirms the passion and continues the dream that Dr. Mears had for making the Bible accessible to everyone. This is a phenomenal resource giving present-day relevance to biblical teaching, especially for moms.

CELESTE PALERMO
Author of *The Coffee Mom's Devotional*

Yielded and courageous, Kathy Pride embodies the essence of God's grace. In *What the Bible Is All About for Moms*, she extends that grace through her sometimes humorous, often delightful and always transparent stories of motherhood. Like an enduring friend, Kathy laughs with you, cries with you, knows you and loves you. She's once been where you are now. You can trust her mentoring as she builds on Dr. Mears's insights, connecting Scripture to life.

ROBIN STANLEY
Publishing Consultant and Coach
Authors' Advocate, Founder and President of o3-free
Board of Directors, CLASSeminars, Inc.

Devotionals help remind us to take a few moments to connect with our amazing God, and Kathy Pride has written a good one! Full of Bible wisdom, humor and stories, this devotional will be a great tool for moms. Pick one up for yourself and the moms in your world!

HOLLY WAGNER
Author of *Daily Steps for GodChicks, Warrior Chicks* and
GodChicks and the Men They Love

A BOOK OF 66 DEVOTIONS

WHAT THE
BIBLE
IS ALL ABOUT
for *Moms*

God's Loving Promises for You and Your Family

KATHY PRIDE

Regal

From Gospel Light
Ventura, California, U.S.A.

Published by Regal
From Gospel Light
Ventura, California, U.S.A.
www.regalbooks.com
Printed in the U.S.A.

Published in association with William K. Jensen Literary Agency, Eugene, Oregon.

Library of Congress Cataloging-in-Publication Data
Pride, Kathy, 1960-
What the Bible is all about for moms : God's loving promises for you
and your family / Kathy Pride.
p. cm.
ISBN 978-0-8307-5160-0 (trade paper)
1. Mothers—Prayers and devotions. 2. Bible—Devotional literature. I. Title.
BV4847.P75 2010
242'.643—dc22
2009051113

1 2 3 4 5 6 7 8 9 10 / 18 17 16 15 14 13 12 11 10

Rights for publishing this book outside the U.S.A. or in non-English languages are
administered by Gospel Light Worldwide, an international not-for-profit ministry.
For additional information, please visit www.glww.org, email info@glww.org, or write
to Gospel Light Worldwide, 1957 Eastman Avenue, Ventura, CA 93003, U.S.A.

To my mom, grandmother and great-grandmother, whose lives have shaped my approach to parenting; and to my children, whom I have the privilege of loving and guiding through life.

Contents

There are many who helped shape this book, and as I contemplated the journey, it struck me that it has been much like a pregnancy, from conception of the idea to the birth of the book. How appropriate for a book for moms!

Many thanks to Kim Bangs from Regal, whose interest and encouragement were instrumental in conceiving this project.

There were many, who like a team of caring and gifted physicians (or midwives!), helped to ensure the health and viability of this project: Bill Jensen, who helped me articulate my thoughts; friends who engaged in debate and support of selected Scriptures to encourage moms; and my family who supported me during times of complications! Special gratitude to my children, without whom I would have no one to mother!

A special thanks to dear friend and fellow writer Connie Pombo, whose watchful and compassionate presence helped deliver the final version. Liked a skilled caregiver, she helped me avoid preterm labor and did not rush to panic when complications arose but maintained a role that ensured everyone's health!

And finally to my Abba Father, who loves me unfailingly.

God's Instruction Book for Moms

"Never will I leave you; never will I forsake you." These words written in Hebrews 13:5 are a wonderful encouragement, especially for moms. After all, God recognized early on that Adam needed a helpmate and gave him Eve, who would become the mother of all the living. Moms obviously played a central role in the Bible from the beginning of time.

As a mom, to know that I am not alone and that God understands and is there with me is a tremendous gift. After all, motherhood is full of new experiences and times when we may feel alone . . . even for moms who have more than one child! God provides His guidance and accompanies us on the journey, at times walking alongside us and at other times carrying us, as we raise our kids.

The Bible is the ultimate parenting manual. There are stories of hope, joy, sadness, tough choices and poor choices—stories in which we can easily see ourselves. What a blessing and relief to know that all trials and triumphs and all challenges and choices are timeless and were experienced by women of faith through the ages. God yearns to share His wisdom and encouragement with us as moms.

Rather than a book of archaic language or rules and regulations, the Bible is a living, dynamic resource that moms can turn to through every stage of the parenting journey. It is never too late to turn to the Bible, and your children are never too old for you to jump in and apply God's Word to your life and theirs. My sons were teenagers before I turned to the Bible and experienced the gems and pearls God had for me. Sometimes the bits of wisdom were obvious, but sometimes I had to dig a bit.

The renowned Bible teacher Dr. Henrietta Mears had a dream and a passion to make the Bible accessible to everyone, and she wrote the Bible handbook *What the Bible Is All About* as a tool to accomplish just that. "Behind and beneath the Bible," she wrote, "above and beyond the Bible, is the God of the Bible. The Bible is God's written revelation of His will to humanity."[1] It was Dr. Mears's desire to help introduce God's Word to as many people as possible. This resource guides new journeyers and well-seasoned travelers alike and has been a companion study tool for many since its first printing over 50 years ago.

This book is the second devotional based on Dr. Mears's book (the first was *What the Bible Is All About for Women* by Lisa Harper). This is a devotional book specifically written for moms, based on Dr. Mears's dream to bring the Bible alive for everyone. It is intended for *all* moms: expectant moms, first-time moms, moms of teens, busy and stressed-out moms (that's all of us, right?), younger moms and older moms, alone moms or moms with lots of (or too much?) support. Wherever you are in your journey, God will meet you there—in the joy, in the bittersweet and even in the sorrow.

My dream is to help you draw a step closer to God and the comfort He can provide through true, real-life experiences that are similar to what biblical moms experienced. All of these stories have been written in a transparent and often humorous tone, and you may recognize yourself in some of them, which will allow the Bible to come alive for you.

This devotional has 66 chapters, each one focusing on one book of the Bible. Take your time and rest in God's Word. Go at your own pace and reflect on one chapter (one book of the Bible) at a time and allow God to speak to you. He will encourage you with His presence, love and understanding.

Each chapter includes the following elements:

- **Snapshot from Henrietta:** This is a basic overview of each Bible book in easy-to-understand language. Any page reference in parentheses refers to Dr. Mears's original book *What the Bible Is All About: NIV Edition* (Ventura, CA: Regal Books, 1998).

- **Mom Moments with Miss Mears:** This section includes verses and passages chosen especially for moms based on Dr. Mears's suggested readings. Because moms are stressed for time and on the go, a smaller sampling of Scripture was chosen from Dr. Mears's original readings.

These readings have been selected specifically with moms in mind to provide encouragement without being overwhelming.

- **Momento:** This is a sentence that sums up how the theme or application from the specific book of the Bible directly connects to moms.

- **Scripture:** This quote from the Bible book describes a mom or a mom-related theme from that book of the Bible.

- **Mama Mia:** This is a devotional story based on the biblical mother or theme.

- **Lightening the Mother Load:** Here you'll find an encouraging concluding thought.

- **Musings for Moms:** This section includes suggested thoughts for reflection.

Read, reflect, enjoy and find your part in God's story!

Note

1. Dr. Henrietta C. Mears, *What the Bible Is All About: NIV Edition* (Ventura, CA: Regal, 1998), p. 15.

E Is for "Eve" and "Epidurals"

Snapshot from Henrietta: "In the *beginning*"—those are the first words of the book of the Bible, Genesis, based on the Greek word for "beginning." How appropriate! The book of Genesis is a book about beginnings: the world, the human race, sin, the promise of redemption, family, civilization, the nations of the world and God's chosen people, the Hebrews.

History and lineage spanning from creation to 1805 BC is packed into this book. Moses served as God's scribe for Genesis, which along with the next four books of the Old Testament make up the Pentateuch, also sometimes referred to as "the Law." Moses fills us in on creation, Adam and Eve's lineage, and the early history of the Hebrew people, including Abraham, Isaac, Jacob, Joseph, and finally the formation of the 12 tribes of Israel. Don't miss the story of Joseph in Genesis 37–49, as he provides the link to the family of Abraham, which birthed the Hebrew nation.

But Genesis is also the story of failure . . . starting with humankind's disobedience to God (which didn't take long to occur) in the Garden of Eden. It is this failure that lays the foundation for the entire Bible: the redeeming work of Christ to bring mankind back into relationship with God.

Mom Moments with Miss Mears

Her Synopsis:
Genesis Portrays Jesus Christ, Our Creator God

Her Suggested Readings:

Genesis 2:7-22	Adam and Eve
Genesis 3:1-24	The fall of humankind
Genesis 13:14-18	The Lord's promise to Abram
Genesis 17:4-8	God's covenant with Abram
Genesis 22:1-18	Abraham's great faith

Momento: The anticipation experienced during pregnancy is un-paralleled. While most of the expectancy is joyful, that *P*-word ("pain") inevitably enters the picture.

Scripture: "I will greatly increase your pains in childbearing; with pain you will give birth to children" (Genesis 3:16).

MAMA MIA

"Congratulations, you're pregnant!" Joy, excitement, fear, trepida-tion, amazement, shock, disbelief, hope—these and other emo-tions all burst from inside a woman's heart when she hears that one sentence that forever changes her life: "Congratulations, you're pregnant!"

I have often remarked that it is no accident that pregnancy is nine months long; it often takes that long to process the myriad of emotions women feel as the day they will meet their baby ap-proaches. Unfortunately, as that day approaches, the excitement of the bambino's arrival may be nudged a bit by the anticipation of labor and the inevitable question of how much it might hurt.

Just remember, God has everything under control.

As much as joy and anticipation are a part of life, pain is too. But hope prevails and is the underlying theme of the parenting manual God has given us in the Bible. The Bible is God's written revelation of His plan for mankind; that despite all that life brings, there is hope and salvation through Jesus Christ. Think about it: If God has a master plan to bring us to Him in relationship, then God certainly can redeem the pain of labor contractions and even transition labor.

Sooner or later in any discussion about pregnancy and child-birth, the topic of pain makes its way to the forefront. After all, pain is something everyone has an opinion about—in fact, often more than one. There are plenty of physiological reasons why women experience pain in childbirth (size and position of the baby, contractions, and fatigue, to name a few); but the Bible points out another reason why women experience pain in childbirth, and that had to do with Eve.

It all dates back to the Garden of Eden. Here's the refresher course: God gave specific directions to Adam (who passed them on to Eve) about not eating from the tree of life in the middle of the Garden. If they did, there would be consequences. And guess what? For women, the consequence became pain in childbirth. Genesis 3:16 says, "I will greatly increase your pains in childbearing; with pain you will give birth to children." Somehow this gets glossed over in childbirth class. "Pain" is a four-letter word that means the same thing as something that hurts. It hurt God that Adam and Eve disobeyed Him, and there were repercussions.

But God also provides a way to soothe the pain. For humanity it is in relationship with Jesus, for laboring women it is anesthesia.

I have to admit when hard labor hit, I wasn't thinking, *E is for "Eve"*; I was thinking, *E is for "epidural."* I had to have one. It was the better way. If God would allow contractions to hurt, then He would provide a way to deal with the pain, and the wonder of epidural anesthesia seemed like the perfect solution. An epidural may not appeal to everyone, but then again not every solution is easy. Women don't tend to really like the idea of anesthesia being administered behind their back through a needle.

God's solution for hope and healing humanity wasn't easy either; it involved the gift of His Son. But look where we would be without it: without hope of a solution—and that is never part of God's plan.

Lightening the Mother Load: God is the great physician and yearns to soothe all pain.

Musings for Moms:
• Pain is a natural consequence of poor decisions. Think of an example from your life. Who suffered pain because of a poor decision that you made?

• Read Genesis 3:1. What technique(s) did the serpent use to fool Eve?

• Genesis 37 begins the story of Joseph (chapters 39–50 recount the rest of his life). The poor guy's life was a series of struggles and bad things. But in every bad thing there is the opportunity for God to redeem what has happened and use it in a good way. Trace a situation from your own life where something bad happened but God used it to help others see and understand His redemption.

The First International Adoption

Snapshot from Henrietta: Genesis left off with how badly humanity had managed to mess up what God had created. Exodus could be subtitled "God to the Rescue." Exodus literally means "way out," and that is exactly what God intended to do: provide the Israelites with a way out of the mess they had made.

We meet Moses, who performed what I call the Moses Dance when summoned by God to lead the nation of Israel. He came up with every excuse in the book for God to give the job to someone else. God prevails and teaches us a valuable lesson: He will equip those He calls to serve, despite human thoughts to the contrary.

Exodus chronicles the crossing of the Red Sea and how God provided protection as the Israelites fled the Egyptian army. God also provided spiritually for this group of grumpy complainers, through protection and guidelines for righteous living. And what thanks did He get? Complaining, moaning, groaning, muttering and the turned backs of people who worshiped a statue of a cow. Finally, Exodus documents the Ten Commandments, the rules for righteous living for humanity, who, if left to their own devices, would have remained in their fallen state of depravity.

Mom Moments with Miss Mears

Her Synopsis:
Exodus Portrays Jesus Christ, Our Passover Lamb

Her Suggested Readings:

Momento: Not all women conceive and raise biological children. Some women become mothers through adoption, like Pharaoh's daughter.

Scripture: "She opened it and saw the baby. He was crying, and she felt sorry for him. . . . When the child grew older, she took him to Pharaoh's daughter and he became her son. She named him Moses, saying, 'I drew him out of the water'" (Exodus 2:6-10).

MAMA MIA

"I'm not waiting any longer to be a mom," my friend Judy announced. Forty-eight and never married, my single friend decided she had waited long enough. In a matter-of-fact tone of voice, her eyes watching me carefully for my reaction, she continued, "I don't need a husband to be a mother. I am going to adopt. I can't wait any longer to bring my daughter home."

I knew Judy had wanted to be a mom for years; she had a wistful reaction when we told her of our own plans to adopt. I remember hoping that someday she would be able to experience the same joy in growing a family through adoption. But she hadn't been ready. She was still holding out hope for a husband. That hope (for a husband) had now been abandoned. "I'm not getting any younger," she continued. "I am ready to be a mom."

"Judy!" I exclaimed, throwing my arms around her and holding her close. "That's wonderful!" And before she could speak, I blurted out my offer to be her travel companion. "You can't go alone," I stated. "If you want I will go with you; I can be your stroller pusher, prayer partner, companion, umbrella holder, and all-purpose friend and child rocker."

In the past, Judy had spoken about traveling to China to bring home a little girl. The number of discarded baby girls in that country was far greater than available forever families. Some babies were abandoned in highly visible places, ensuring their survival; but others were discovered in more obscure locations, some even abandoned by rivers as Moses had been.

"I am working with an agency that has a little girl in an orphanage in China. She is three and has a minor heart defect." And then she reached into her purse and pulled out a photograph. Two big brown eyes gazed at me from the picture. Her forehead was framed by straight dark bangs; her hair put up in two lopsided ponytails with red hair ties. She was clinging to a ragged teddy bear. "Soon she will have more to hug than just a teddy bear," Judy whispered.

"She's beautiful," I said softly. I thought back to when I had first seen my own adopted daughter's picture. I had the same feelings now as I looked at Judy's waiting child and imagined mother and daughter meeting for the first time. Anticipation and memories suspended me in a magical state, reminding me that God has a place for every child in His family and had provided the model for adoption early on in the story of His people.

I thought momentarily about the selfless gift of love the birth mother had made in protecting her child by leaving him or her in a place where he or she was certain to be found. It was the first step that would lead to being adopted into another family and having a new life.

International adoption isn't anything new. It goes all the way back to the time of Moses. It is a timeless truth and provides hope to birth moms, waiting moms and children.

Lightening the Mother Load: We are all invited to be adoptees into God's forever family.

Musings for Moms:
- Read Exodus 2:6. What emotion did Pharaoh's daughter feel? Does God hold the same sense of compassion for us? How does God provide guidance for us through His compassion?

- Do you know (or are you yourself) an adoptive mom? Can you imagine loving your child any differently (or more) if he or she were a biological child? Do you think there is any difference in the degree that an adoptive mom or a biological mom loves her children?

- Think of a time when you were selected to do something for which you felt woefully inadequate. How does the story of Moses encourage you? Read Exodus 4:12.

Getting Rid of the Guilt

Snapshot from Henrietta: Rules, rules and more rules—that is what Leviticus is all about. There are rules for how to keep the rules to "get right" and "keep right" with God. And there are "get right" offerings and "keep right" feasts.

Here's a clue though: No way, no how, can any of us possibly observe all the laws and regulations, some of which are "do" and some of which are "don't." There are just way too many—617 to be exact. But rather than bogging us down, they are meant to be liberating, pointing us to Christ, whose perfect life and death on the cross make us completely holy—both body and soul. Dr. Mears writes, "Leviticus is a timely book, for it insists on keeping the body holy as well as the soul. It teaches that the redeemed ones must be holy because their Redeemer is holy" (p. 58).

Rather than developing legalistic rigidity (which leads to a self-righteousness and a "holier than thou" attitude), we are able to embrace freedom through Christ.

Mom Moments with Miss Mears

Her Synopsis:
Leviticus Portrays Jesus Christ, Our Sacrifice for Sin

Her Suggested Readings:
Leviticus 16:29-34   Day of Atonement
Leviticus 26:1-13   Reward for obedience

Momento: Guilt. All moms suffer from it sooner or later. The good news is that Christ is our guilt offering. No revisiting required!

Scripture: "The LORD said to Moses, 'When a person commits a violation and sins unintentionally in regard to any of the LORD's holy things, he is to bring to the LORD as a penalty a ram from the flock. . . . It is a guilt offering'" (Leviticus 5:14-15).

MAMA MIA

"Guilt"—unfortunately it is a word that is alive and well in every mom's vocabulary.

Our kids have the most talented way of embarrassing us mothers publicly at the most inopportune times and places. The result is that we often don't feel like we measure up (to an impossible standard) and worry about what others (especially other moms) think.

The truth is that it really only matters what God thinks. And He understands. He has provided the guilt offering through the gift of His Son. We make mistakes, but Jesus, the guilt offering—God's gift—atones for our sin. Pretty cool. But we still beat ourselves up.

Not too long ago I took my daughter swimming, and there were other kids in the locker room giving their mom a real run for her money. The other mom's two daughters were trying to lock each other in lockers, chasing each other and dodging their mortified mother. The younger daughter was successful in locking her older sister in a dressing room and stood defiantly facing her mother, who couldn't catch her from the other side of the locker-room bench. The older sister was screaming from the changing room, the younger sister had a smug look of satisfaction spread across her face, and the mother was trying to cajole without hissing or hitting. I raised a silent prayer of thanksgiving that today it wasn't me in the other mom's shoes. I had worn them before.

My daughter Nicole watched the escapade (one she could have written the script for) from under the hair dryer. Her partner-in-crime sister happened to not be with us, sparing me from possibly being a participant in the same scenario.

"We've all been there, you know," I offered. She gave me a weak smile, not at all convinced.

"Really," I said. I told her how on a recent trip to an ancient cathedral my daughter had defiantly run away from me in a large courtyard just as a monk made his way up the stairs and gave us both a rather pointed look. I told her how I had felt like crawling into a hole and how guilty I felt for the ungodly thoughts I had about my abilities as a mom and how to handle discipline. I suspected the other mom could relate. Talk about guilt . . . and embarrassment.

When we are confronted with mortifying situations (that typically are more distressing to us than to bystanders), God is delighted to meet us in that place—if and when we invite Him in. He already knows about the shenanigans anyway and has already taken care of them for us. The good news (literally the translation of "gospel") is that the guilt offering came as part of the package deal when we accept Jesus. No more wallowing in guilt. No more room for guilty self-flagellation. The old adage "let go and let God" is the perfect guilt offering. So even though we may feel guilty, we need to let it go and let God.

Lightening the Mother Load: The tendency to feel guilty is a part of life; part of our new life in Christ is the fact that our guilt offering has already been made.

Musings for Moms:
- Write a prayer to combat mother guilt.

- Have you responded to mistakes in your own life with grace or condemnation?

- Contemplate how Jesus has rewritten the rules for your life by eliminating guilt offerings.

God's Way: The High Way

Snapshot from Henrietta: Numbers chronicles the 40 years the Israelites wandered in the wilderness following their liberation from Egypt. It highlights the good, the bad and ugly: the goodness of God's provision to a grumbling and cantankerous group, the bad things they were saved from, and the ugliness of their unappreciative hearts. They just didn't get it; God saved them over and over, and they never once said "thank You."

Finally, they understood that they were saved to serve God. But in the meantime, they got caught up in selfishness. They kept thinking they would have been better off if they had just stayed put back in Egypt. Numbers is also the log of their desert-time travels with Moses at the helm. They walked in circles for 40 years before finally getting to the Promised Land a generation later. Numbers chronicles the Kodak moments as well as the images of the trip from you know where.

Dr. Mears reminds us that God provides everything, and that is still true today: "Here were about three million people on a sterile desert, very little grass, very little water, and no visible means for support. How were they to be fed? God was there! How were they to trace their way through a howling wilderness where there was no path? God was there! God's presence provides everything!" (p. 72).

Mom Moments with Miss Mears

Her Synopsis:
Numbers Portrays Jesus Christ, Our "Lifted-Up One"

Her Suggested Bible Readings:
Numbers 9:15-23   The cloud above the Tabernacle
Numbers 14:17-18   Generational sin
Numbers 22:1-41   Balaam

Momento: Mumbling, grumbling and one-upmanship—rather than trying to have the last word or keep score, we need to yield our lives to God.

Scripture: "Miriam and Aaron began to talk against Moses because of his Cushite wife, for he had married a Cushite. 'Has the LORD spoken only through Moses?' they asked. 'Hasn't he also spoken through us?' And the LORD heard this" (Numbers 12:1-2).

MAMA MIA

How many moms fall prey to maternal one-upmanship? I don't like to be compared to others, so why do I fall into that trap myself? I hate to admit it, but if the confessions of a control-freak mother were exposed, doing things my way and creating a good impression are part of my story. Ever been there? It's nothing new (there is nothing new under the sun). The same story has been around since the time of Moses.

What better grid to use to measure how we're doing than the infamous holiday letter? But instead of encouraging other moms, these embellished versions of American family life can end up being more of a downer, and as children of God we are to be ambassadors of hope.

There was a time the annual newsy letter I wrote (and the many I still receive) read more like a résumé suitable for framing than a year in the life of an average American family. "The girls continue to participate in many activities, including swimming, tumbling, dance, softball and Girl Scouts." Honor roll, All-Star team selection, piano recitals, toe-shoe debuts and every other imaginable accomplishment were shared.

The letters were fictional, though, and didn't really honor God. I had tired of reading them, so why was I still writing them? I would have preferred the nonfiction version that included transparency, encouragement and hope; so my annual letter changed.

Now even if my news isn't the best, I choose to share those life stories as encouraging messages of walking the life journey of a mom with honest understanding, often sprinkled with humor.

"The girls don't always get along, but a tender moment happened recently. Our older daughter stayed home sick from school and missed her first day of school all year. She was bummed because she really wanted to make it through the year without missing a day. Instead of rubbing it in, her younger sister drew a personalized 'certificate' honoring that desire."

Relish the everyday moments. Share gratitude. And join me in setting a new standard for the holiday letter, one that honors doing things God's way.

Lightening the Mother Load: God knows us intimately—both our struggles and our successes—and loves us deeply. We don't need to put on an act.

Musings for Moms:

• Reread Numbers 12:1-2. Of what were Miriam and Aaron guilty? Have you found yourself in the same frame of mind?

• Think of a time when God illuminated your own tendency to share information with a self-serving spin. Why do we sometimes have such a difficult time recognizing this inclination to share information with the embellishment of an over-positive spin?

• Read Numbers 22:21-41. How did God teach Balaam that there is more to figuring out a situation than what we see? How can you apply this to your life?

Morning, Noon and Night

Snapshot from Henrietta: Deuteronomy, the last book of the Pentateuch (the five books of Moses), is a book of remembrance. "Deuteronomy" means "second law," and in this book, Moses gives a final set of instructions to the people of Israel. The book also contains a collection of Moses' orations and songs.

Moses had been entrusted with leading the people out of Israel, and now as his earthly life was coming to a close, he grabbed one more opportunity to guide his people. He clearly outlined the blessings of obedience and the curse of disobedience. He instructed the Israelites, "Look back, look up, and look out." He told them to look back over the past 40 years and realize the journey should only have taken 11 days. Talk about foot blisters . . . and the culprit? Unbelief. Then Moses reminded them to look up to the one true holy God of Israel for guidance.

Finally, Moses urged them to look out and ahead to the blessings of obedience. Deuteronomy winds down with a warning about disobedience and closes with the succession of Joshua upon the death of Moses.

Mom Moments with Miss Mears

Her Synopsis:
Deuteronomy Portrays Jesus Christ, Our True Prophet

Her Suggested Bible Readings:
Deuteronomy 1:10-11	Blessings
Deuteronomy 5:1-33	The Ten Commandments
Deuteronomy 30:1-20	Prosperity after turning to the Lord

Momento: Mothers carry a responsibility to teach and equip their children. Faith is one of those areas. God's voice will direct us.

Scripture: "Love the LORD your God and . . . serve him with all your heart and with all your soul. . . . Fix these words of mine in your hearts and minds. . . . Teach them to your children, talking about them when you sit at home and when you walk along the road, when you lie down and when you get up" (Deuteronomy 11:13,18-19).

MAMA MIA

Parents are responsible for teaching their kids all kinds of things, but one of the most important is about having a relationship with God. Some of the ways we nurture this relationship are through prayer, service and love.

Moms have an amazing opportunity to influence their children in areas of faith, using their own life as a textbook.

I remember a recent conversation with my friend Katy. We agreed that Sunday School and Hebrew School are great (Katy's husband is Jewish); but to make God's love real to them, kids need to understand prayer, service and love in practical and age-appropriate ways.

Our conversation continued and Katy told me about a time she walked her son, Ben, home from school when he was in kindergarten. It was a daily ritual that took them on a path that circled a small lake that was situated between the elementary school and their home, creating a sanctuary for ducks, geese, chipmunks, squirrels and other critters. It was a nature preserve in their backyard and, as such, was the perfect setting for conversations about God and His world and a transition from school to home.

Ben and his mom talked about all kinds of things during those walks, but Katy remembered one conversation in particular. It was a fall day and the air was just starting to turn cooler. Katy and Ben were about halfway home when Ben pulled his jacket close around him and climbed up on a tree stump with the authority of an accomplished orator. He pulled his jacket a little tighter and looked up at the sky.

"Ben, what are you doing?" Katy asked.

And still looking at the sky, following the V formation of a group of Canadian geese, he answered, "I am talking to God."

He continued to stand, silently talking to God, and Katy stood and waited until his conversation was over. She understood that he was engaged in a real conversation, the conversation of prayer.

When he was finished and stepped off the stump, Katy commented to Ben that he had been praying; that prayer was simply a conversation between him and God and was just one way in which he could communicate with Him. Nothing complicated. She paused while he absorbed what she had just said; and they talked a little more about God: loving Him, talking to Him and serving Him.

I nodded in agreement and added my own experience, which had left its mark on my girls. I recalled a time when we had been out in the car and passed a guy holding a sign that simply said "Hungry." He appeared to be in his twenties, the same age as their two older brothers (who were not hungry).

Instead of going directly to our destination, I chose a detour to McDonalds, where I bought a meal to share. I circled around and then pulled over and paused to have a conversation with the young man, asking him about his story. The girls absorbed the dialogue and the effect the gift of a simple meal had on him.

Later we were able to talk more about the opportunity and how it tied in with Jesus' command to feed those who hunger. I shared that in addition to feeding his belly, we were also able to feed his soul by serving him. And they understood.

God provides lots of opportunities to share our faith with our kids in uncomplicated ways that are part of the natural ebb and flow of our lives.

Lightening the Mother Load: The way we live teaches our children about loving and serving God; actions speak louder than words.

Musings for Moms:

• List three ordinary situations that you can use to teach your child about God.

• Is your life a testimony to faith in God? In what ways do you model service to your children?

• Read Deuteronomy 11:22-23. What command is tied to this promise? Translate this command and promise into a practical example from your life.

R Is for "Restoration"

Snapshot from Henrietta: The book of Joshua picks up where Deuteronomy left off and begins the second division of the Old Testament, the books of History. Joshua opens with the Lord commanding Joshua, Moses' successor, "Moses my servant is dead. Now then, you and all these people, get ready to cross the Jordan River into the land I am about to give to them—to the Israelites. I will give you every place where you set your foot, as I promised Moses" (Joshua 1:2-3).

Dr. Mears comments, "No book has more encouragement and wisdom for the soldier of the Cross than this book of Joshua. It is full of spiritual truth" (p. 89).

Joshua is divided into the conquest of the Promised Land (chapters 1–12) and the occupation of the Promised Land (chapters 13–24). What Moses started, Joshua finished. Read about the fall of Jericho and how obedience to God led to victory (Joshua 5:13–6:26). Next draw encouragement that a prostitute (of all people!) was among God's chosen servants in this story, showing us that we are not to be defined by what we are but by who we are.

Mom Moments with Miss Mears

Her Synopsis:
Joshua Portrays Jesus Christ, Captain of Our Salvation

Her Suggested Bible Readings:

Joshua 1–2	Leadership and legacy is passed on
Joshua 3:1-17	Crossing through turbulence with God's help
Joshua 6:1-27	Marching orders from God

Momento: Don't allow someone's reputation to determine your opinion of him or her.

Scripture: "So they went and entered the house of a prostitute named Rahab and stayed there" (Joshua 2:1).

MAMA MIA

There are times when a woman's reputation may precede and/or define her, but God is in the life-transformation business and will take the experiences of your life and allow them to be used for His glory. "God is always doing the impossible. God's biddings are His enabling" (p. 95).

I was looking forward to going to my twenty-fifth high-school reunion, and I was especially looking forward to seeing my friend Cindy (not her real name). Cindy had become an influential leader in her field and was a gold mine of great stories about God and what He was doing in and through her. Her outrageous experiences had to be true; one couldn't make up the stories she told. She shared openly and with a passion that revealed her *joie de vivre*.

I dialed her number, eager to make plans to get together at the upcoming event. I couldn't wait to see her.

"Cindy, how are you? It's so good to hear your voice. I can't wait to see you at the reunion," I said, managing to cram all the words into one breath.

"I've decided not to go. I just don't want to revisit that time in my life." She paused, sighed and then continued, "I know that was then and many years have passed, but I just can't shake my past." Her answer saddened and disappointed me. Cindy had a reputation with the boys in high school that still haunted her.

"But, Cindy," I said softly, "you're not the same person. Look at how God is working through you." Cindy served in a leadership position at her church and loved sharing innovative and creative ideas about serving God in ways that were inviting and inclusive (in particular to hurting women). Her smile was contagious and, well, she was fun!

"I know . . ." she said, pausing, "but I just don't want to see any of the people that remind me of that time." She couldn't bring herself to face any of the people (including some of those "boys" and their wives) who might still think of her as "that promiscuous girl"—having forever labeled her without giving her the opportunity to redefine herself.

I imagine Rahab felt the same way. It seems like every time we read about the poor girl, her name isn't mentioned without the descriptive label "prostitute" attached. "Rahab the prostitute." For a long time when I read Rahab's story, I got hung up on the label rather than on how God used her and the fact that God *did use* her. What an encouragement!

The truth is, we all make mistakes—many mistakes—but God is in the mistake-correction business. In fact, God uses all our life experiences, including our mistakes, in preparation for the work we do in service to Him. "We are just a part in a mighty whole. Do your little part" (p. 91).

Like Rahab, Cindy was uniquely qualified to serve God. And He used her experiences for His purposes. Her life choices and experiences provided her with empathy and understanding to reach a specific group of God's people.

God has a special place for all of us in loving and serving others. Don't let past mistakes define you or someone else.

Lightening the Mother Load: God will use all of our experiences, including mistakes, to serve and glorify Him. Our part is to share.

Musings for Moms:
- Is there something from your past that has left you with an unfavorable or uncomplimentary label? Do you believe God has the power to redefine who you are?

- Do you know anyone with a "bad" reputation? How do you treat that person? Why?

- Have there been times in your life when God has used a mistake you made to help others and bring Him glory?

Infertility Treatment My Way!

Snapshot from Henrietta: Judges, the book of the Israelites slip-sliding away. And it didn't take long. Judges picks up after Joshua and the elders who had served the Lord had died. "In those days Israel had no king" (Judges 17:6), and it remained so for the next 350 years chronicled in this book.

During this time, things went from bad to worse. Not only was there no king, but there was also no integrity. Rampant moral decay and disobedience were prevalent at every turn. Dr. Mears tells us that "the book is full of rebellion, punishment, misery and deliverance" (p. 109).

During this time, the people were ruled by 14 judges whom God raised up to deliver His oppressed people. But guess what? Like spoiled children who want their own way and think they can do it better themselves, the Israelites didn't listen, and their disobedience led to ruin. "It [the book of Judges] is filled with struggle and disasters, but also with the moral courage of a select few" (p. 106). Despite the depravity of humanity chronicled in this book, hope always prevailed.

Mom Moments with Miss Mears

Her Synopsis:
Jesus Christ, Our Deliverer Judge

Her Suggested Bible Readings:

Judges 2:16-23	There will always be those to encourage
Judges 6:1-16	God will remind us of His miracles
Judges 15–16	Obedience brings miraculous power

Momento: God's ability to achieve miracles still exists. We just need to depend on Him for them.

Scripture: "A certain man of Zorah, named Manoah, from the clan of the Danites, had a wife who was sterile and remained childless. The angel of the LORD appeared to her and said, 'You are sterile and childless, but you are going to conceive and have a son'" (Judges 13:2-3).

MAMA MIA

God specializes in the impossible. How cool is that? In fact, the more impossible, the more God delights in accomplishing it. But there are conditions: God operates on His own timeline, He longs to bring us to a place of expectancy, and He deserves the glory when He achieves the impossible.

The gauntlet of impossible challenges is one that is difficult for solution-driven women to ignore. There is something about being told something is impossible that summons us to engage in conquering it, sometimes at too much cost. Have you ever felt that way?

According to *my* timeline of my perfectly laid-out life, the time to conceive the third child I had waited so long for had finally arrived. Since I hadn't had any trouble getting pregnant with my older children, I assumed it would be easy again this time.

But I was wrong. God had something else in mind, and I wasn't very good at listening to His voice. So I took matters into my own hands and tried to help things along by accelerating our journey by going through infertility treatment. Have you ever tried to give God a hand?

Not long after we started treatment, I got pregnant. Elated, I told everyone. Three weeks later I miscarried. Instead of leaning on Him, I retreated into a solitary place and months of continued treatment without the desired outcome. The only words I heard were, "We don't know why you can't get pregnant . . . it's just not possible."

But this time, instead of languishing in that place, I heard God whisper to my soul the words that Jesus spoke in Matthew 19:26: "With man this is impossible, but with God all things are possible." God led me to a place of surrender to Him and expectancy that in His time, in His way, He would bring a child to us.

Ultimately I yielded as God brought me to a deeper place of surrender, and I spoke the words my husband had been waiting for me to share: "I'm ready to give up the dream of being pregnant. I just want to be a mom. Let's adopt." Relief spread over his face; he had been ready to grow our family through adoption for months. So we initiated the process.

Nine months later, just like a pregnancy, God allowed us to bring home our daughter from Vietnam. We held our daughter and reveled in each new day with her. "Afraid it's just not possible . . . just not possible." Those words hung in suspension in the back recesses of my mind; yet I always hoped that if it fit God's plan, someday we would achieve the impossible and conceive.

Time passed and I had a chance to travel to Europe with my parents. I packed my young daughter up and went with them, but I missed my older boys so desperately that at the last minute I decided to change my return flight home. I wanted to get home a day earlier, but that flight was sold out. Two days earlier was available, so I rearranged my plans.

God brought me home two days sooner than I had planned for a reason. He knew the time was finally right for me to be pregnant one more time. Our older daughter was secure in our forever family, a sense of quiet expectancy for God to work in our family in His way had settled in me, and I was thankful to God for growing my family. That night God made the impossible possible and our youngest daughter was conceived.

With God nothing is impossible. "We find the patience of God and His constant readiness to respond to the least sign of penitence in His people" (p. 111). I just needed to allow the impossible to happen in His time.

Lightening the Mother Load: God yearns to achieve the impossible and fulfill our hopes and dreams. We often don't understand what God is doing in our situation, and what He is doing may not line up with our expected solution, but He always wants what is best for us. Our walk of faith may not be easy, but it will give Him the glory.

Musings for Moms:
- Read Judges 2:10-14. What happened? Why did it happen? Can you think of a similar example from your own life when you were disobedient to God?

- What happens when you take matters into your own hands? Is it smooth sailing, or is the journey usually full of bumps?

- Think of what happens in your own family when there is no leader. Is it calm or chaotic? How is this similar to the time described in Judges when there was no king and everyone did as he or she saw fit?

Mother-in-Law Blessings

Snapshot from Henrietta: The book of Ruth establishes the lineage of David, a direct ancestor of Christ. But Naomi, Ruth's mother-in-law, is also a central figure in this book. Naomi had a tough life. She and her husband lived among the Moabites (away from the Israelites) for many years and had two sons. After her husband died, the sons grew to adulthood and married. The women they married didn't share their heritage rooted in God (even though the Israelites weren't following God at the time).

When her two sons then died, Naomi was left alone with her two daughters-in-law who didn't share her faith. Despite Naomi encouraging them to move on and build their own lives, one of the two, Ruth, stayed with her. Together, they returned to Judah, where ultimately Ruth came to worship the God of Israel and to marry Boaz, Rahab's son (yes, Rahab, the prostitute). She was the great-grandmother of David.

Ruth is a wonderful story full of hope during an otherwise pretty hopeless time in Israel's history. It is full of evidence of God's abundant grace.

Mom Moments with Miss Mears

Her Synopsis:
Ruth Portrays Jesus Christ, Our Kinsman-Redeemer

Her Suggested Bible Readings:
Ruth 1–4   Family ties bring hope

Momento: There are times when the mother-in-law and daughter-in-law bond is stronger than the mother-daughter bond.

Scripture: "But Ruth replied, 'Don't urge me to leave you or to turn back from you. Where you go I will go, and where you stay I will stay. Your people will be my people and your God my God'" (Ruth 1:16).

MAMA MIA

"Hey, Nancy!" I called across the dock to my sister-in-law who had joined us at the lake with her two grandchildren, who were squealing with delight.

"Hey what?" she answered back, chasing the kids and squirting them with water guns, the fun audible and visible.

Abby and Jacob continued to shriek as their grandmother played with them. They all wore sand pails on their heads as helmets; it was hilarious. I thought about how lucky Sharon was to have Nancy as her mother-in-law.

Nancy's mother (my mother-in-law) and I had always gotten along, but we did not have a deep bond. Our love for each other was held together by our common love for her son, my husband. It was not the deep bond of connection that Naomi and Ruth had shared.

"Nancy, what was your mother-in-law like?" I asked.

Nancy's answer was swift and decisive. "Oh, Kathy . . . she was wonderful . . . absolutely wonderful. When the boys were little, she took them one weekend a month, so Steve and I could have some alone time together."

She paused and seemed to get lost in the memories of past years. Now she was caring for her grandchildren in the same way, giving her son and his wife the same gift of couple time.

"Marge, my mother-in-law, was amazing. She used to take the kids down to a local pond where they would feed the ducks. There was one in particular that they named Uncle Wiggly. And I remember there were two swans at the lake they called Gus and Gutsy. The boys still talk about it. . . ." her voice trailed off. "I know my boys cherished their time with their Grandma Marge. I want my grandkids to have great memories of their time with me, their Grandma Froggy."

It was apparent that Marge had been like Naomi to Nancy, embracing her as her own daughter, and now Nancy was doing the same with Sharon. It was beautiful to see the legacy of the relationship that God had provided. It gave me a window into the type of relationship I hope to have with daughters-in-law, if that comes to pass in my life.

Ruth's commitment to her mother-in-law was off-the-charts deep. Ruth chose to accept Naomi's faith and her way of life. Rather than returning to the pagan Moabite culture of her youth, she chose to adopt a new home, family and God—forever. And God rewarded Ruth by redeeming her past and bringing her into a full life, which included her place in the lineage of King David and Jesus.

Just as Boaz (a relative of Naomi's) was Ruth's kinsman-redeemer, first bringing Ruth into his family and then into God's family, God does the same with us. He is our kinsman-redeemer. This is, as Miss Mears says, "God's grace. He adopts the Gentiles into God's family" (p. 117).

Lightening the Mother Load: God brings all of us into relationships with others; we honor Him when we value and nurture those relationships, especially those with family.

Musings for Moms:
- When is the last time you thanked your mother-in-law for the gift of her son in your life?

- Read Ruth 1:16 again. If your husband died, would you go live with your mother-in-law and never leave?

- What blessings came to Ruth by staying with Naomi?

1 SAMUEL

Read My Lips!

Snapshot from Henrietta: First Samuel opens a new period of biblical history, that of the kings. It is the first of six books that chronicle kings in Israel's history. The 300-year history of Israel's rule by the judges came to an end with Samuel, a really good guy in a really bad time. He became Israel's spiritual leader, but the Israelites really wanted a king. Bad move. Instead of having God as their king, as intended, they wanted a human king like the surrounding nations had. And a king they got—and not a very good one at that. Dr. Mears points out, "We either can have God's best or His second best, His directive will or His permissive will" (p. 124). So the Israelites exercised their permissive will and ended up with a disastrous king. Samuel, on the other hand, was a spiritual giant born to a godly woman, Hannah. It was Samuel who anointed David king. But David was God's choice, not the people's choice.

Mom Moments with Miss Mears

Her Synopsis:
First Samuel Portrays Jesus Christ, Our King

Her Suggested Bible Readings:
1 Samuel 1:9-19	Hannah's prayer
1 Samuel 2:1-11	Hannah's Song
1 Samuel 15:22	Listening for the Lord's voice
1 Samuel 16:4-9	Doing what the Lord says

Momento: God's hearing is perfect; He is just a whisper away.

Scripture: "As she kept on praying to the LORD, Eli observed her mouth. Hannah was praying in her heart, and her lips were mov-

ing but her voice was not heard. Eli thought she was drunk"
(1 Samuel 1:12-13).

MAMA MIA

I can relate to Hannah. I suspect many of us can. What I love about this woman is that she wasn't afraid to cry out to God, and she wasn't afraid to thank Him when He answered. Her passion didn't go unnoticed or unrewarded.

It didn't go unnoticed by Eli, the priest, either, who misjudged her. But Hannah corrected him.

Anguished moms can appear to be crazy or even drunk. Have you ever been there? I have, and God met me in that place and answered my desperate plea for hope and comfort.

I recently experienced one of those times when onlookers probably would have assumed I was either stark raving mad or drunk. My lips were moving as Hannah's had, and just like her I "was pouring out my soul to the LORD" (1 Samuel 1:15). And then when He answered, I burst into tears.

On this particular occasion my prayers weren't as a mom, but as a daughter who had recently lost her dad, and I missed him. I had been overcome by sorrow that seeped out of my heart and through my lips.

I was in New York, and it was a beautiful day, unseasonably balmy for February.

I walked across town to see the art gallery where my dad had fallen. God knew I wasn't ready to go in the gallery—fortunately, the doors were locked and the shades drawn—but I paused and sat on the front steps for a few minutes, "speaking" to my dad, an artist who both appreciated and created. I desperately yearned to feel his presence and was thinking about a particular piece of artwork he had done when I was a kid.

He was illustrating for Lord and Taylor at the time, and he always worked in the studio in our apartment. I became particularly enamored with one job that included a pair of Bedlington terriers. Bedlingtons aren't your run of the mill dog—they sort of resemble sheep. (In fact, I haven't seen one since I was 10.)

Not long after the ad ran, someone involved with the Westminster Dog Club sent my dad a note complimenting him on having truly captured the personality of the dog. The representative was convinced that our family owned one. I wish! We tried to convince our dad to get one, but no amount of begging on our part worked. However, we did enjoy an afternoon together at the great dog show at Madison Square Garden.

As I sat on the gallery steps that balmy February day, I allowed the memories of that particular time to comfort me, yet I wanted more. I stood up and crossed the street, my lips still mouthing my request to God to bring my father to me. I continued, walking and talking, when for some unknown reason, I turned and glanced over my shoulder. There, out of the corner of my eye, I spotted a man walking his dog. And it was a Bedlington terrier.

Even though others might have thought I was drunk or crazy, God knew differently and answered the prayer of an anguished woman.

God will meet you in those places. He knows your heart. He won't judge you, but He will send you His healing touch. Don't be afraid to call out to Him. He is waiting to answer.

Lightening the Mother Load: Abandoning your desperation and crying out to God open the door to miraculous answers.

Musings for Moms:

• Reflect on a time when you were in desperate need of God's touch.

• Read 1 Samuel 1:10. Can you identify with the emotion of bitterness that Hannah felt? How did you respond to such a feeling?

• Take a moment to write your own prayer of thanksgiving to God.

"Bath"—Is That for "Bathing" or "Bathsheba"?

Snapshot from Henrietta: Second Samuel is the story of David's life. While David was one of the greatest leaders in all of human history, there are two key things that are encouraging about his life for us: (1) David was a shepherd before he became king, and (2) he messed up—big time. But God used him anyway, reminding us that He can and will use all of us to serve His purposes.

David stumbled plenty along the way. He fell for another guy's wife, slept with her, and she got pregnant. David tried to cover it up by bringing her husband home to be with his wife, but Uriah, Bathsheba's husband, didn't think it would be right to be with his wife (as in make love to her) when so many others couldn't (being away fighting the war and all). So David figured he didn't have a choice but to arrange for the poor guy to be knocked off in battle.

Shirking on his kingly duties to serve in battle, committing adultery and then arranging a murder were all part of David's bio. Yet he repented and loved God with all his heart, and God used him as a mighty leader and part of the direct lineage of Jesus. He also had a vision for rebuilding God's Temple (accomplished during the lifetime of his son Solomon), led many military victories, and saw the return of the Ark of the Covenant to Jerusalem.

Mom Moments with Miss Mears

Her Synopsis:
Second Samuel Portrays Jesus Christ, Our King

Her Suggested Bible Readings:

2 Samuel 2:1-4	God provides direction when we inquire of Him
2 Samuel 5:1-4	God can equip young leaders
2 Samuel 11:1-27	David's sin
Psalm 51:1-19	Create in me a pure heart

Momento: Let God be the one to soothe a lonely heart.

Scripture: "One evening David got up from his bed and walked around on the roof of the palace. From the roof he saw a woman bathing" (2 Samuel 11:2).

MAMA MIA

What was Bathsheba doing taking a bath where someone outside her house could see her anyway? Didn't it occur to her that she might be noticed? Didn't she draw the curtains so no one would see her? Or was that the point—that she wanted to be noticed? Maybe she was lonely and dying for attention. If we're honest, I think we've all visited the lonely hearts club once or twice.

It's hard work being a mom, and there are times when our kids can drain us, regardless of how old they or we are. Being up all night with a baby, toilet training a toddler, singing "The Itsy Bitsy Spider" for the seventeenth time, relearning third-grade math to help with homework, soothing hurt middle-school feelings, dealing with dating rejection . . . the list goes on. Even moms of adult kids can be drained and lonely—it's just different (and usually involves money).

Before paying a visit to the lonely hearts club, seek a more satisfying alternative that's available but often overlooked: the renewal that is available when we turn to Christ with our fatigue, sorrow, pain and loneliness. He understands and, as the lover of our soul, He will fill our lonely heart to overflowing with His love and peace. Unfortunately, we usually attend a pity party or two and look for love in all the wrong places first.

My mind wandered to one of my friends who had suffered from loneliness and had done the equivalent of dipping her toes in a bathtub open to outside viewing. My friend Diane (not her real name) came over one time for coffee and wanted to talk. She wistfully remembered when she and her husband had first dated, and she had felt like the center of his world.

"I haven't always felt lonely," she said, before telling me tales of youthful flirtatious rendezvous full of daring fun (that had admittedly at times gone too far) that had been a regular part of their relationship. She knew her smile did things to him; things that made him behave in ways that made her heart race. But now he came and went, mostly to work, and he didn't laugh much, especially with her.

She paused in front of a mirror as we moved from the kitchen to the family room. She glanced over her left shoulder, first eyeing her waist, then her hips and finally the silhouette of her body down her long, graceful legs. Twins hadn't robbed her of her figure.

"Not bad for a mother of twins," she commented, more for her own benefit. "Why doesn't he notice? I don't look like a frump, do I?" But she already knew the answer. Surely there was another man who would find her attractive and whose attention would soothe her lonely heart.

Before long, Diane found out there were plenty of guys who would lavish her with the kind of attention she was hungry for. She saw no harm in inviting some attention, as long as she kept it at arm's length. But it didn't satisfy her for long.

"I got a little bit carried away the other day. It was fun, but I got scared when he invited me to join him for another cup of coffee at his place," her voice trailed off and I moved forward in my seat, concerned that she had accepted the invitation.

"I didn't go, though. I realized that like the words of the song we listened to when we were younger, I was 'looking for love in all the wrong places.'"

"I'm glad you didn't," I said, my eyes locking with hers as I listened while she unburdened her soul, relieved that she was ready to accept that God, not men, would heal her hurting heart.

"Me too . . . me too," she said, her eyes acknowledging the truth of God's love for her.

I understood her loneliness. But I also understood that Jesus is the only One who could quench her soul's lonely thirst. Thankfully, she realized this as well.

Lightening the Mother Load: God yearns to satisfy your longing for complete love. He will fill you in a way that no person can.

Musings for Moms:
• Read 1 Corinthians 10:12-13. How do these verses relate to this story? How should we respond when we're tempted to do something we know is wrong?

- Have there been times when you have invited attention from someone you shouldn't have? How did you deal with the situation?

- Are you lonely? Do you feel alone? Why? What can you do to change the way you feel?

If I Can't Be the Mom, No One Will!

Snapshot from Henrietta: The book of 1 Kings could be subtitled "History 101" ("History 102" can be found in 2 Kings). Originally, 1 and 2 Kings formed one book. But when the original book, which had been written in Hebrew, was translated to Greek, it was too long to fit on one scroll and needed to be split between two (as also happened with 1 and 2 Samuel and 1 and 2 Chronicles).

First and 2 Kings span 400 years. First Kings opens with King David and continues with the story of his son Solomon. Both kings ruled during a period of growth and stability. King Solomon's wisdom was unmatched, but after his death, the country went downhill. The subsequent kings were foolish, selfish and subpar. Israel decreased in size and the Temple was burned to the ground. The decline from glory to ruin skidded to an end with the king of Babylon.

First Kings concludes with the life and times of Elijah, one of God's prophets who kept trying to tell the backsliding kings what they needed to do to get it right. But they were so adamant in their refusal to listen that poor Elijah just felt like curling up and dying. He even asked God to put him out of his misery (see 1 Kings 19:4). But God wasn't quite finished with Elijah (a good thing for the Israelites), and the "rest of the story" (to use the Paul Harvey phrase) can be read in the remaining chapters of 1 Kings.

Mom Moments with Miss Mears

Her Synopsis:
First Kings Portrays Jesus Christ as King

Her Suggested Bible Readings:
1 Kings 10:1-29   Wisdom and blessings
1 Kings 17:1-24   Blessing and obedience—the story of Elijah
1 Kings 18:1-46   More of Elijah's story

Scripture: "The king said, 'This one says, "My son is alive and your son is dead," while that one says, "No! Your son is dead and mine is alive." Then the king said, 'Bring me a sword.' So they brought a sword for the king. He then gave an order: 'Cut the living child in two and give half to one and half to the other'" (1 Kings 3:23-24).

Momento: God's wisdom is always available to us; we just need to ask (see 1 Kings 3:9; James 1:5). The problem is, we usually don't.

MAMA MIA

I glanced at the caller ID and picked up the phone with trembling hands. The adoption agency worker said the next time she called, she would have information about our daughter; she was just waiting for the email from Vietnam.

"Hello?" my voice squeaked in anticipation. Was today the day I had been waiting for? Would I finally get more information about my daughter, born halfway around the world? Up until now, all we knew was that there was a baby girl born sometime, somewhere in a far-away land, but we had no specifics. That was all about to change.

"Kathy!" Andrea's voice overflowed with excitement. "We have a baby for you! She was born November 15 in the northern part of Vietnam." She continued speaking, but I didn't hear the next few words. My heart stopped when I heard the date: November 15. My daughter's birthday, but also a significant date I had tried to bury for years.

I listened as Andrea continued. "Her birth mother was only 19 and in poor health. She had the baby in the hospital—quite unusual, really. Your daughter was taken to the social protection center directly from the hospital where she is being taken care of until you bring her home."

November 15. My mind traveled back almost 20 years to that date during my freshman year of college. It was the date my first child's life had ended through abortion. I had rationalized the choice; how could I give my child to another mother by choosing the life-honoring option of adoption? That was too hard, too much of a sacrifice. It was simply easier to snuff out a life. Or so I thought. I consulted only my own sensibilities, which were selfish and shortsighted, rather than embrace God's wisdom.

I quietly thanked God for our daughter's birth mother. She made the selfless and life-giving choice of allowing another mother to nurture and raise the child who had grown in her womb.

And I thanked God both for the gift of His Son and for the gift of His grace and forgiveness extended to me through the improbable but divinely arranged intersection of two mothers, two choices and one date.

Lightening the Mother Load: God's vision and wisdom are infinite and encompassing, unlike human shortsightedness. God always knows the *big* picture and will redeem our mistakes. Let us go to Him.

Musings for Moms:

- What does David acknowledge in 1 Kings 1:29? Do you believe there is a connection between repentance and blessing? What is the connection in this verse?

- How might gratitude and forgiveness be connected?

- In times of need, where may we hear God's voice? Read 1 Kings 19:11-12.

Mouth to Mouth

Snapshot from Henrietta: Second Kings ("History 102") continues where 1 Kings left off. History 102 is pretty bleak, with the exception of the story about the prophet Elisha (introduced in 1 Kings 19), Elijah's trainee, in chapters 2–8. Other than that, Israel's story is full of corruption and plunder, all the consequences of their inability to learn to depend on and obey God, something He yearned for. In this history lesson, we learn of Israel being split into two regions, Judah in the south and Israel in the north. The picture is bleak: Israel falls to Assyria, and Babylon crushes Judah, kicks its people out and then destroys the Temple. Oh my. Things went from bad to worse, but Elisha did have some really bright spots in chapters 5 and 6.

Mom Moments with Miss Mears

Her Synopsis:
Second Kings Portrays Jesus Christ as King

Her Suggested Bible Readings:

2 Kings 2:1-22	Elijah and Elisha
2 Kings 17:7-23	The consequence of disobedience

Momento: Sacrifice is part of being a mom.

Scripture: "Then he got on the bed and lay upon the boy, mouth to mouth, eyes to eyes, hands to hands. As he stretched himself out upon him, the boy's body grew warm" (2 Kings 4:34).

MAMA MIA

"Sacrifice." It is a word that embodies what moms do.

Mothering is hard work. I'm not sure how many of us would willingly apply for this job if we really had a clue of the enormity of what it entails.

Each parenting stage provides its own set of challenges, requiring its own set of sacrifices and expressions of love. Some are physically exhausting, some emotionally so. All provide opportunities to learn about and grow in caring. And in loving sacrificially. After all, sacrifice and service are true expressions of love. God's gift to us of Jesus is the model.

Ponder the following characteristics of sacrificial love and how Jesus provided the model for us in loving our children in both the big and little things in life:

S Selfless: There is no more selfless gift than giving up one's life. Jesus did this for us and we can give of ourselves to our children when we seek first to nurture them and meet their needs physically, emotionally and spiritually.

A Adore: God loves us unconditionally. God is love. I try to love my children unconditionally, but I fall short in this area too. "For all have sinned and fall short of the glory of God" (Romans 3:23). Sin . . . the separation from God. We have all been there.

C Comfort: Jesus comforts us, so we can comfort others. We each have unique experiences and hurts; and God will comfort us so we can in turn comfort others, including our children. "The Father of compassion and the God of all comfort, who comforts us in all our troubles, so that we can comfort those in any trouble with the comfort we ourselves have received from God" (2 Corinthians 1:3-4).

R Rescue: God has rescued us, and through the years we will have several opportunities to rescue our children. We may snatch a teetering toddler from falling into a dangerous place; a young child from bullies; a teen from bad influences; a young adult from poor life choices. All may yield a more abundant life.

I Intercede: The Holy Spirit intercedes for us. "In the same way, the Spirit helps us in our weakness. We do not know what we ought to pray for, but the Spirit himself intercedes for us with groans that words cannot express" (Romans 8:26). As a mom I know how to groan! And sometimes that will be how I also intercede for my kids.

F Faithful: God is faithful. What a great model, that no matter what, God "is faithful in all he does" (Psalm 33:4) and "will not forsake His faithful ones" (Psalm 37:28). We may not always agree with the decisions or choices our kids make, but we are to remain faithful in love.

I Indescribable: Just as it is difficult and elusive for a mom to describe the love she has for her newborn baby, God's love for us is also indescribable.

C Caring: God cares about us. He even knows the number of hairs on our head (see Matthew 10:30). So we also care intimately about our children—their wellbeing, their hopes and their dreams.

E Entrust: God gave His Son for us. He entrusted Jesus with ensuring our eternal wellbeing. Children likewise are a gift from God, and we are entrusted with caring for and raising them.

When I view sacrifice through the lens described above, I am filled with a sense of gratitude for the gift of God's love and the privilege of passing it on.

Lightening the Mother Load: Sacrifice is hard; it does not come naturally. Allow Jesus to be your role model.

Musings for Moms:

· Has there ever been a time when you were asked to give something up and you didn't think it would be humanly possible? How did you react? What did you learn?

· What is the most sacrificial thing you have ever done?

· In 2 Kings 17:14, the people of Israel are described as "stiff-necked." Think of a time you were stiff-necked. Did it have to do with being asked to do or give something up that you didn't agree with? Did being that way do you any good?

Purpose with a Plan, Not Plan with a Purpose

Snapshot from Henrietta: First Chronicles starts with history, and I mean a *lot* of history. And genealogy, too. It is thought that this book was written by Ezra after the Israelites returned from captivity in Babylon (450–430 BC). The majority of the book reads like volume 2 of King David's biography, emphasizing the protection and blessing that come when a leader is anointed by God. It is just one more example of God's grace toward the people of Israel. Dr. Mears adds, "Through such books as the Chronicles we get the history of the Jewish nation. Through this nation our Lord came to earth. God chose this people for the fulfillment of His great promises and purposes" (p. 154).

Mom Moments with Miss Mears

Her Synopsis:
First Chronicles Portrays Jesus Christ as King

Her Suggested Bible Readings:
1 Chronicles 13:1-14   Discerning God's will
1 Chronicles 16:7-36   Giving thanks
1 Chronicles 28:1-21   Pursuing purpose

Momento: We can plan all we want, but God's purposes will prevail.

Scripture: "Consider now, for the LORD has chosen you to build a temple as a sanctuary. Be strong and do the work" (1 Chronicles 28:10).

MAMA MIA

I never set out to be a writer. I didn't even study English or journalism in college. But God had other plans for me, and believe me I tried very hard to run the other way. Funny how that goes . . .

Have you experienced a time when God specifically called you and you responded by pointing out to God that He had most certainly made a mistake (by the way, God never makes mistakes) and that there was absolutely no way you were the right person? That's how it was at first with me and writing. I performed a great rendition of what I refer to as the Moses Dance (also known as the Jonah Jig).

"Who me, God? You want me to do what? To write a book? But I'm not a writer . . . well, uh, I know I have a story to tell, but be a writer?" I even tried Moses' excuse that I was "slow of speech and tongue" (Exodus 4:10). "Not me, I'm not qualified. I'm not sure what I would write . . . okay, an article maybe, but a book?"And I kept dancing, solo. All to no avail.

When I first came to Christ, I believed beyond a shadow of a doubt that I was to serve God by volunteering with a local Pregnancy Care Center. Why? Because I was eminently qualified. I had experienced crisis pregnancy, was an OB nurse and childbirth educator, and was a mom to three birth children and an adopted child. Who could possibly be better qualified to serve? But it wasn't about me—and that was the piece I was missing.

Then God called me to write. I wasn't quite as eager to follow that purpose, but slowly I released my grip of false understanding (and my plan) and started to be His scribe and dance as His partner. I realized that God had chosen me to share a unique message based on experiences I had gone through. God called me to write the book I had needed to read, and He revealed His truth "that in all things God works for the good of those who love him, who have been called according to his purpose" (Romans 8:28). Called according to *His* purpose, not *my* plan. I was a slow learner. And when I forgot that this wasn't about me, He reminded me.

And then the hard work began. God was faithful and supplied the tools. And He will do the same for you. Listen for Him to call you and then be prepared for the hard work ahead. God equips moms for the jobs ahead.

Lightening the Mother Load: We all have a unique purpose in serving God. He knows what it is and will equip us with tools and strength to succeed for Him.

Musings for Moms:

- Can you think of a time when you danced the "Moses Dance" in response to a request from God?

- The prayer of Jabez is found in 1 Chronicles 4:10. Do you believe that praying this prayer may "enlarge [your] territory"? Can you think of an example from someone's life that illustrates this?

- What is something that you felt totally unprepared for in your life but God equipped you to do?

Admitting When You're Wrong

Snapshot from Henrietta: Second Chronicles picks up where 1 Chronicles left off and serves as its sequel. First Chronicles provides biographical details about King David, while 2 Chronicles tells the story of his son Solomon. Solomon was a wise king, asking God to bless him with more wisdom and knowledge. "God appeared to Solomon and said to him, 'Ask for whatever you want me to give you.' . . . 'Give me wisdom and knowledge, that I may lead this people, for who is able to govern this great people of yours?'" (2 Chronicles 1:7-10). God was pleased with Solomon's request and granted him great wisdom . . . and more! Things were finally looking up for the people of Israel. This book parallels what is written in 1 and 2 Kings.

Mom Moments with Miss Mears

Her Synopsis:
Chronicles Portrays Jesus Christ as King

Her Suggested Bible Readings:
2 Chronicles 15:1-19   Seeking and finding God
2 Chronicles 20:1-37   Remember the battle belongs to the Lord
2 Chronicles 30:6-9   Don't be stiff-necked; return to God

Momento: Admitting when you're wrong is one of life's toughest challenges.

Scripture: "If my people, who are called by my name, will humble themselves and pray and seek my face and will turn from their wicked ways, then will I hear from heaven and will forgive their sin and will heal their land" (2 Chronicles 7:14).

MAMA MIA

"Will you forgive me? Please?" I asked my adult son, the tears gently slipping down my cheeks.

"Mom, we've talked about this before; of course I will. Think how many times you have already forgiven me." Matt stepped toward me, placed his hand on my forearm and then drew me toward him into a deep embrace. I felt the tension release from my body. And the tears slid more freely down my cheeks.

"Thank you . . . thank you," I said, the second time the words barely audible. I stepped back and locked eyes with him.

We shared a long, silent connection; we had been to this place before and its familiarity was soothing.

There had been times I didn't want to forgive; and the same had also been true for him. Trust had been fractured and it took a long time to rebuild. We stumbled often on the path of healing, sometimes slipping backward, but more frequently moving ahead, even if at times only in baby steps.

We advanced when we humbled ourselves and asked each other for forgiveness, discarding the need to have the final word. We stumbled and backslid when we forgot to forgive and allowed pride and selfishness to establish itself front and center, hurling hurtful words at each other like grenades that would explode and forever leave wounds as sharp as those inflicted by embedded shrapnel.

Admitting when we are wrong, apologizing and asking forgiveness shows our kids that we are also human and not above the standard that Jesus set for us and that we expect of them.

Practicing humility and forgiveness in *all* situations where they are merited—not only the "big" ones—opens the gates to God's presence. And I can't think of any place I would rather be.

Lightening the Mother Load: Forgiveness invites God to enter our pain and apply the healing balm of His love to our hurts.

Musings for Moms:
· Do you think it is a sign of strength or a sign of weakness to ask for forgiveness?

- What does 2 Chronicles 7:14 say? Do you believe those words?

- Think of a time when you spoke words you wished you could retract and haven't been able to apologize for. Take a moment to make a phone call or jot a note apologizing for that time.

Not Following the Rules

Snapshot from Henrietta: The books of Ezra and Nehemiah were combined in the Hebrew Bible. Both books tell the story of the return of God's Chosen People from their 100-year-long exile in Babylon, one of the most important events in Jewish history. The book of Ezra looks both to the past and to the future. In this book we find the second exodus for Israel, the exodus from Babylon (the first one was from Egypt). Like Moses before him, Ezra was a leader chosen by God to deal with Israel in both a strong and a merciful way. The look to the future shows God giving the Israelites a foothold in Jerusalem to rebuild His city. The overriding message of Ezra is that God does not forget His people.

Mom Moments with Miss Mears

Her Synopsis:
Ezra Portrays Jesus Christ, Our Restorer

Her Suggested Bible Readings:

Ezra 1:1-11	Stolen items returned
Ezra 4:1-4	Times of opposition
Ezra 1:10-17	Confession of sin

Momento: Leaders need to set a good example; there are consequences when they don't.

Scripture: "After these things had been done, the leaders came to me and said, 'The people of Israel, including the priests and the Levites, have not kept themselves separate from the neighboring peoples with their detestable practices. . . . They have taken some of their daughters as wives for themselves and their sons, and have mingled the holy race with the peoples around them. And the leaders and officials have led the way in this unfaithfulness'" (Ezra 9:1-2).

MAMA MIA

There is no getting around it: Rules are a part of life. We don't always like to follow them, sometimes we don't understand them, but sooner or later if broken, consequences follow. This is as applicable to moms as it is to high-profile leaders.

As moms, when we suffer the consequences of broken rules, our restoration comes from Christ. Focus on the "rest" in "restoration"; the rest comes from abiding in and with Him and doing what we know He would approve of.

We have all broken rules that separate us from God. No matter *how* much we may try to rationalize or justify our choice, wrong is wrong, and often the most significant consequence is the poor example it sets for our children, the leaders of the next generation. This may start innocuously enough, but if left unchecked, it could lead to bigger and bigger infractions. Generally speaking, the bigger the broken rule, the bigger the consequence.

"Mom, can we stop and buy some candy at the Dollar Tree to take to the movies?" my youngest daughter chirped from the back seat.

Sooner or later I was going to need to stop this habit. There was a sign in plain English in the theater that read, "No outside food or drink allowed." There wasn't too much wiggle room in that statement. Yet I ignored it time after time.

"We're not supposed to, but Mom never paid attention to that rule before," editorialized my older daughter. She was right. I had officially opened the door to sliding down a slippery slope.

"No, not anymore; it's against the rules," I said with confidence in my voice, firmly establishing my position.

"Oh, come on, Mom. You always do," my younger daughter begged, her chirp turning into a whine.

"No. No more," I stated, reinforcing my decision. "We're not doing it anymore. From now on we will get popcorn there instead."

That seemed to satisfy my daughters and also satisfied my desire to do what was right and set a good example.

It wasn't long afterward that a high-profile leader slipped from grace and my daughters picked up on the story. It gave us an opportunity to talk about the importance of always following rules, because sometimes a small pattern of mistakes escalates, and big mistakes can lead to really big consequences.

The hypocrisy that characterized the leader's choices was magnified, and I was thankful that I had been restored to God's way before the "little" rules I broke had grown larger.

It was also an opportunity to talk about the restoration that is available to all of us through God's grace—a gift available to moms and high-profile leaders alike. Look what God did in Ezra's time. It is no different today.

Lightening the Mother Load: God's grace is always available and larger than our mistakes.

Musings for Moms:
- Do you consider yourself a leader? If so, what group(s) do you provide leadership to?

- What qualities do you believe make up a good leader?

- If leadership equals influence, then how important do you believe your leadership position is within your family?

Doing the Right Thing

Snapshot from Henrietta: Nehemiah tells the story of the Chosen People returning to Jerusalem. Ezra is also the author of this book, although it is based on the writing of Nehemiah, who led and orchestrated one of the biggest building projects undertaken to date, that of rebuilding the wall around Jerusalem. When the Israelites returned to Jerusalem, they came back to a sorry, sorry state. It looked as if three category 5 storms had swept through, back to back, each one leaving more ruin and destruction in its wake. So just as there had been grumbling with Moses earlier in the Israelites' history, there was some grumbling this time too . . . different issues, same grumbling. But Nehemiah was a superbly skilled leader and prayer warrior, and he led the people through the successful rebuilding of the wall around Jerusalem.

Mom Moments with Miss Mears

Her Synopsis:
Nehemiah Portrays Jesus Christ, Our Restorer

Her Suggested Bible Readings:
Nehemiah 1:5-11   Nehemiah's prayer
Nehemiah 5:1-12   Doing what is right
Nehemiah 8:10   The joy of the Lord

Momento: Try to let your kids work out their own solutions, but if something is blatantly wrong, step in.

Scripture: "So I continued, 'What you are doing is not right. Shouldn't you walk in the fear of our God to avoid the reproach of our Gentile enemies? I and my brothers and my men are also lending the people money and grain. But let the exacting of usury stop!'" (Nehemiah 5:9).

MAMA MIA

"No, Mom, please . . . don't say anything," Nicole pleaded, her expression communicating a mix of anxiety, confusion and embarrassment.

"Honey," I explained patiently for the seventeenth time, "I have to this time. It just isn't right."

Nicole also knew it wasn't right, but she still didn't want me to say anything. But I knew I had to. The line had been crossed. It was part of my maternal duty to defend my daughter.

I didn't remember this degree of "mean girlness" from my childhood. When I was eight, I played Barbies for hours and watched shows on TV that now air on Nick at Nite. But somehow today's generation was different.

One little girl had told several untruths about Nicole to her classmates that resulted in ostracism and contempt, not to mention alarm on the part of their parents. Now Nicole was coming home from school every day in tears because the other girls believed the lies. There was no way I could simply let this go. Aside from Nicole's devastation, what if someone called the police?

"I'm sorry, Nicole, but I need to talk to the guidance counselor. She will know what to do."

"But, Mom," she said, her eyes growing wider and her voice trembling. She knew I meant business.

It didn't take long to correct the issue. The other little girl admitted she had made the stories up and apologized. Before long the girls were playing together again during recess.

God is a model parent and allows us to live our lives and learn how to become problem solvers, but He is also there to protect us when things tip out of balance. We can lean on our Father in heaven to give us guidance about how to restore balance with our children.

Lightening the Mother Load: Moms walk a parental tightrope, teetering between grace and enabling, hoping to help and sometimes striving to solve. If we fall, God is there to catch us and set us back on the right path.

Musings for Moms:

- How hard do you think it was for Nehemiah to follow God's call? Think of a time when you were called by God to do something. Was it hard?

- Just because Nehemiah did the right thing didn't mean that he didn't meet with resistance. Do you think all leaders come up against resistance? Why or why not?

- Are you willing to step out in faith and lead in a situation, even if it isn't the popular choice? When have you had to do this with your children?

The Right Place at the Right Time

Snapshot from Henrietta: The story of Esther is a cross between an incredible adventure about being in the right place at the right time (God-ordained, of course!) and a happy-ending love story. Esther was a Jewish orphan who became a Persian queen. Go figure. One additional tidbit of information is that "Esther" means "star," which she certainly was to the Jewish people.

The book opens with a description of an opulent party thrown by King Xerxes of Persia at a time the Persians were planning an expedition against Greece. The party went on for seven days and included the who's who of Susa on the invitation list. While King Xerxes was doing his thing, his wife, Vashti, was entertaining the Persian women. But she humiliated the king when she refused to come to him at his beck and call, and she was given the boot.

Fast forward. Esther became Xerxes' queen, giving the Jews prestige at the court, which ultimately made it possible for Nehemiah to rebuild the wall around Jerusalem. Who'd have thought . . . well, God, that's who! In an intricate story of intrigue designed to destroy the Jewish people, we learn that God placed Esther front and center as the one who came to Persia "for such a time as this" (Esther 4:14) and foiled one bad guy's plot big time. In fact, the plan backfired on bad guy Haman and ultimately led to his hanging. Talk about plotting, suspense and victory for the underdog!

Mom Moments with Miss Mears

Her Synopsis:
Esther Portrays Jesus Christ, Our Advocate

Her Suggested Bible Readings:
Esther 4:1-17   For such a time as this
Esther 9:20-22   Turning sorrow to joy

Momento: Being in the right place at the right time cannot be underestimated.

Scripture: "And who knows but that you have come to royal position for such a time as this?" (Esther 4:14).

MAMA MIA

Jennifer was looking forward to meeting her friend and former coworker Sue for lunch. It had been a couple of months since they had gotten together, and today Jennifer knew that Sue, who had a joyful and caring disposition, would provide just the company and comfort she needed as she continued to struggle with infertility treatment. Jennifer was still processing the news she had received from her doctor that her last in vitro fertilization cycle had not been successful. Three years of infertility treatment, 10 years of marriage, and no baby.

Sue arrived and leaned in to kiss Jennifer on the cheek. "Jennifer, it's so good to see you! It has been way too long."

Sue and Jennifer had worked together for years as partners in the same law firm before Jennifer had left to become the county district attorney. They had a comfortable friendship, the kind of relationship where they could pick up the conversation right where they had left off, no matter how much time had elapsed from the time they had last spoken together. Soon the conversation turned to the one thing Sue really wanted to discuss with Jennifer.

"So, Jennifer, how are you doing with the infertility treatment? Are you still hoping to be a mom?" Sue asked tentatively. Despite being close, it was still a sensitive topic. "I hope you don't mind my asking," she added quickly.

"Funny you should ask," Jennifer answered. "I just found out yesterday that my last treatment cycle didn't work. We don't have any more options at the clinic, so I guess we're done," she answered, her voice quivering while she desperately tried to hold back tears.

Sue listened and then continued. "Well, maybe not. My daughter is pregnant and has decided to give the baby up for adoption. She's due in six weeks. I thought that maybe you and Jeff would be interested in meeting my daughter and talking to her about adopting the baby."

Jennifer sat in silence, trying to absorb the enormity of what Sue had just said. Jen and her husband, Jeff, had thought about adoption but didn't know where to begin. She couldn't believe her ears. A possible opportunity to bring a baby home . . . God opening a door just as another had closed.

"I will absolutely talk to Jeff; we'll let you know," Jennifer answered, a feeling of hope filling the void that had been created by her doctor's news.

Sue and Jen continued to share, daring to express the hopes and dreams that God could fulfill for both families through a carefully orchestrated set of people and events . . . for such a time as this.

They parted after lunch, and it was only a few days later that Jen and Jeff met Sue's daughter, Kristie. God evaporated any feelings of apprehension that had existed and He shaped the individuals into one family as Kristie chose Jennifer and Jeff to be her baby's parents.

Three weeks later, three weeks before her due date, Kristie gave birth to a healthy baby girl. And Jen and Jeff were able to be there when their daughter was born; Jeff was even able to cut the umbilical cord. What had seemed like an impossible situation had changed almost overnight.

The timing and circumstances of Jen's quest for motherhood had been designed for such a time as this, which is so often God's way: to bring together a seemingly unlikely group of people or circumstances to achieve His will.

Lightening the Mother Load: Although we may not always understand or agree with what happens, God always has a plan and His timing is perfect. We simply need to trust Him.

Musings for Moms:
- Have there been times when you have experienced the providence of being in the right place at the right time to excel in leadership?

- Do you believe that everything happens for a reason? Why or why not?

• Think of a time when you were faced with a problem to which you thought you had the answers. Did it work out the way you thought it would?

You Fool!

Snapshot from Henrietta: The book of Job is a training manual for how to deal with trials, pain and suffering. The book of Job is also a book of exquisite poetry, the first of the next five books of the Bible that tell of the experiences of the heart. Despite being a masterful book of poetry, the subject matter is depressing.

Tested. Tested to the extreme, Job suffered from just about every affliction possible, including plummeting from prosperity to poverty, losing all his children, and being struck with a horrible and painful skin disease from top to bottom. His wife cursed him and called him a fool, and his friends who came to comfort him couldn't believe their eyes when they saw him. Yet through all of this, Job never gave up believing in God and in His sovereignty.

The two major themes of the book of Job concern questions that we still ask today. Why do bad things happen to good people? After all if God is such a wonderful God, why does He allow the incredible suffering that some people experience? And how should God's people respond to pain and suffering? Like Job, or like Job's wife? Job hangs in there and ultimately gets answers and restoration from God.

Mom Moments with Miss Mears

Her Synopsis:
Job Portrays Jesus Christ, My Redeemer

Her Suggested Bible Readings:
Job 1:1-22	Bad things happen to good people
Job 2:1-13	There is no testimony without a test
Job 37:23-24	Encouragement and promise
Job 42:1-6,10	The Lord's redemption

Momento: Bad things happen to good people. Despite this, it is possible to love and praise God through heartbreak and sorrow.

Scripture: "His wife said to him, 'Are you still holding on to your integrity? Curse God and die!' He replied, 'You are talking like a foolish woman. Shall we accept good from God, and not trouble?'" (Job 2:9-10).

MAMA MIA

We have friends who have been through heartbreak and loss. They have said more than once that they can identify with Job's pain. But that is not what they focus on. What they focus on is God's love and promise to bring redemption. Their faith is steadfast and illuminates a wide path along the road of hope that they share with many.

I met Myron and Mary Ellen King through my husband, who was their dermatologist. He took care of their first baby, a son named Derrick who was born with epidermolysis bullosa (or EB for short), a devastating genetic skin disease. There are many variations of EB, a blistering disease, but Derrick was born with the worst kind.

Despite being told there is no cure for EB, the Kings held out hope that their son would be spared from the ravages of the unfamiliar disease they were carriers of. They nurtured, loved and cared for Derek while they held on to the hope that he would beat the odds. Unfortunately, his condition deteriorated, and Howie and I both knew it wouldn't be long before we received the phone call telling us of Derek's death.

"Hello? It's Myron King. Is Dr. Howard there?" I answered the phone and yelled for Howie. I knew in my spirit that Derrick's time had come.

I handed the phone to Howie and left the room. I waited to go back into the bedroom, until I no longer heard the muffled sounds of conversation. No words were necessary to know what Myron had shared.

Howie stood and stared out the window, tears first forming in his eyes and then slowly spilling down his cheeks. He held on to the bedpost and bit his upper lip, trying to hold back the tears that were now flowing freely.

Yet through their pain, Myron and Mary Ellen never stopped loving God.

Several months passed before we spoke with the Kings, and the next call we got from them was to share the exciting news that Mary Ellen was pregnant, and they were ready to welcome another baby into their home. Their joy was tempered by the knowledge that they had a one in four chance of giving birth to another baby with EB, yet they remained excited and hopeful.

Shortly after their second son, Jensen, was born, they learned that he also had EB. Despite the eventual loss of their second child, their faith in God never wavered, and their continued love and faith in God, even when bad things happened, made an indelible impression on many people.

More months elapsed and they conceived one more time. Mary Ellen gave birth to a third son, who also was affected by this devastating disease. Yet their faith never wavered and they continued to be a remarkable living testimony to submitting to God's plan, difficult as that might be.

"How?" I asked. "How do you hold on to your faith and not give up on God? How do you hang on like Job, your faith remaining steadfast?"

"It isn't always easy. Some days are really hard," Mary Ellen said, her voice trailing off.

I appreciated her honesty and knew it was a difficult subject for either of them to talk about. But I also knew that not a day went by that they didn't think about and miss their boys.

Myron remained silent for a moment, tears filling his eyes. "I miss my boys terribly, but I know I will see them again, and I have said that if even one person comes to know Jesus through them, then the sacrifice will have been worthwhile."

Talk about faith. They were living it daily.

Mary Ellen paused, sighed and then commented, "I'm not there yet. But I just have to trust and *will* trust that God has His reasons. I think I can identify with Job," she concluded with a rueful laugh. "Some days are easier than others."

The conversation I had with them was inspirational. Now whenever I meet people who share the perspective Job's wife had (to curse God, rather than to praise Him), I gently share elements of the Kings' story. I don't have the answers any more than Myron, Mary Ellen or Job did, but like them, I also choose to claim God's promises.

Faith sustains. It is "being sure of what we hope for and certain of what we do not see" (Hebrews 11:1).

Lightening the Mother Load: Even during times of immense sorrow or pain, God will never leave us or forsake us. If we feel distanced from God, it is the result of *our* walking away from Him.

Musings for Moms:

· What is the most difficult situation God has allowed in your life?

· Do you believe that sorrow can be a part of God's plan in your life?

· Have there been times your faith in God has faltered? How do difficult circumstances affect your faith or the faith of others?

Delight and Disappointment

Snapshot from Henrietta: The book of Psalms is a collection of 150 poems, just under half attributed to King David as author. Many of the psalms have praise as a central theme. In fact, the Hebrew name for the book of Psalms is "Praise." Dr. Mears cites Psalm 29:2 as the key verse to the book of Psalms: "Ascribe to the LORD the glory due his name; worship the LORD in the splendor of his holiness." She also notes, "Every psalm is a direct expression of the soul's consciousness of God" (p. 197). The book of Psalms has something for everyone. They are poems of joy, poems of mourning, poems of wrenching honesty, and poems of sorrow and of praise. No matter where you are in your life, there is a psalm that will seem like it was written just for you.

Mom Moments with Miss Mears

Her Synopsis:
The Psalms Portray Jesus Christ, Our All in All

Her Suggested Bible Readings:

Psalm 1:1-6	The path to blessings
Psalm 19:1-14	Praise for God
Psalm 37:4,7; 42:1-2,5	Key encouragements
Psalm 139:13-14	God created you and your children

Momento: There will be both times of delight and disappointment with our kids.

Scripture: "Sons are a heritage from the LORD, children a reward from him" (Psalm 127:3).

MAMA MIA

God's parenting model is based on unconditional love. I am certain as His child that there are times when I both delight and disappoint Him. But regardless of my behavior, His love for me is unceasing.

Sometimes when I sit and ponder the love God has for me, I have a hard time wrapping my arms around it. It is so vast, and I know that even though it is how I am called to love my own kids, there are times I am really bad at it. My ability to love rises and falls according to the barometer of my kids' delight or disappointment mode.

As moms, we have all experienced moments of delight and disappointment. And if we're honest, we find it is easier to accept our kids as a reward when we're delighted in them. (Truthfully, I find it a bit easier to love my kids when they delight me.) However, we still need to value and cherish them as God's heritage (and reward), even when they are a disappointment.

I find this has become more challenging as my children have grown older. I believe part of the reason for this is that the older our children are, the more they exercise their free will. Consequently, they don't always make the best choices! A "borrowed" pencil in third grade doesn't carry the same parental disappointment as copying the answers on a high-school exam, underage drinking or infidelity in a relationship. But the delight and love we show our kids are still the same and are unerring because they are based on the truth of God's Word.

Recently I was experiencing a down moment, disappointed in a choice one of my daughters had made. I called my friend Janet, whom I admire tremendously, and asked her how she continued to be a living example of gentle grace with her friends and her children. Despite choices her adult son had made that cost him his relationship with his wife and daughter, Janet always speaks of him kindly, with the tenderness of a soft caress in her voice. She is sadly aware of the choices that have resulted in broken relationships, yet she always extends grace and love to everyone—her son, Jay, included.

"Janet, how do you do it? How do you just not shake Jay when he continues to make the same choices that cost him his family?" I could learn a thing or two (more like ten!) from Janet, so I was perched on the edge of my seat, eager for her answer. It was simple, and I actually already knew what it was. It just had slipped away momentarily.

"I just remember that as much as I love him, God loves him more," she said. She paused a moment and then added, "Loving and delighting in God help me stay focused on how His love can flow through me. I couldn't do it without God's love and power . . . my own love isn't always enough."

I appreciated her honesty, and her words brought me back to God's Word. As Dr. Mears pointed out, "The more you read the Word, the more you want to. As one great Christian leader has said, 'The gospel feeds you, then it makes you hungry.' It never grows stale. You cannot read it too often or too much" (p. 200).

Love the LORD your God with all your heart and with all your soul and with all your strength (Deuteronomy 6:5).

Delight yourself in the LORD and he will give you the desires of your heart (Psalm 37:4).

Through loving God, He will bless you with the ability to love and communicate that love to your children in both times of delight and disappointment.

Lightening the Mother Load: See others through God's eyes, as unique individuals with wonderful potential, even when you are challenged by disappointment.

Musings for Moms:
- Which do you point out more frequently to your kids: delight or disappointment?

- How do Psalms 32:10 and 147:11 describe God's love? How does God's love compare to the love you feel for your kids?

- Why is it better to concentrate on future possibilities than on past failures?

The Perfect Woman

Snapshot from Henrietta: The book of Proverbs is God's guide for practical living. Commonly referred to as the book of wisdom, it was penned by King Solomon. Remember him? He was King David's son, the one who asked for God to grant him wisdom. And he was nice enough to write this wisdom down for us so that we could have this handy reference guide! And timeless, too, even though it was written long, long ago.

Proverbs transcends time in providing practical counsel. Throughout Proverbs we read about the results of both wisdom and foolishness. The book ends with Proverbs 31, a chapter that Dr. Mears refers to as "a chapter about women's rights" (p. 209), but one I refer to more as a description of supermom, one who does it all: wife, mom, wage earner (CEO, probably), crafter, outreach worker, ministry leader, seamstress, cook—a multi-tasker who never rests a minute yet still manages to have a sense of humor. So open up to Proverbs 31 and read about this amazing woman!

Mom Moments with Miss Mears

Her Synopsis:
Jesus Christ, Our Wisdom

Her Suggested Bible Readings:

Proverbs 2:1-6	Seeking wisdom
Proverbs 3:1-6	Acknowledging God
Proverbs 4:23	Guard your heart
Proverbs 15:1	Being gentle
Proverbs 31:10-31	A woman ahead of her time

Momento: The Proverbs 31 woman is the original Martha Stewart! But how many moms succeed in meeting multiple roles and demands?

Scripture: "Many women do noble things, but you surpass them all" (Proverbs 31:29).

MAMA MIA

It wasn't until I read Dr. Mears's commentary on Proverbs 31 that I developed a new appreciation for the Proverbs 31 woman:

> The book [of Proverbs] closes with one of the most beautiful chapters in the Word. . . . This is a chapter about women's rights. "Give her the reward she has earned, and let her works bring her praise at the city gate" (v. 31). Wherever Christ goes, womanhood is lifted up. . . . In Christian lands, woman is equal to man (p. 209).

I don't know about you, but in the past I generally got depressed after reading Proverbs 31. I will let you in on a little secret: I am domestically challenged and always got a little bummed after reading about a woman who could do it all. And this woman could do it all. She was incredible. She was a shrewd businesswoman, mother, cook, seamstress and buff babe all rolled into one. And she did it all without the modern conveniences I have at my disposal, so what's my excuse?

I do love Dr. Mears's commentary. No doubt she was ahead of her time (like the Proverbs 31 woman), and at least her assessment of the Proverbs 31 woman didn't leave me feeling quite so defeated. Yet I suspect it is a place we have all been. Most of us know someone who just seems, well, too perfect.

Since cooking isn't my forte, women who have the gift of being quintessential culinary queens always seemed to get under my skin. Instead of cheering them on and appreciating my own gifts, I allow myself to feel beaten up by their successes.

I recall one unfortunate experience in particular. Keep in mind that Julia Child and Martha Stewart weren't my mentors, and, I repeat, I am not much of a cook. Even though I worship at a Mennonite church, I grew up in New York City. I do not know the first thing about gardening, and I do *not* grow and can my own vegetables (although I did try once and ended up selling all the stuff at a yard sale). But I do like to bake.

So anyway, said perfect woman hosted a Halloween party, and I saw the cutest recipe for a cake in one of the women's magazines. It was complete with cracker gravestones, gummy bats and Cool Whip ghosts. I decided to make this cake and take it (with pride) to the party. Pathetic as it was, I was quite pleased with myself.

When I arrived at the party, I discovered that a couple of my gummy bats had lost their wings, the cracker gravestones had crumbled (just an antique touch, I rationalized), and my ghosts looked more like blobs. Yet I was still fine with my cake creation until the hostess brought her dessert out to the table and put it next to mine. And it was the same cake. Except her bats were flying all over, her ghosts didn't require CPR, and her gravestones even had writing on them, penned with chocolate icing.

I burst into tears and escaped to the bathroom to have a good cry and blow my nose. In my mind, she was perfect and I was a failure. Of course, neither was true. Our value wasn't in who could produce the prettier cake but in the fact that we both loved God.

We both could have learned a thing or two from our role model in Proverbs 31. Women can be leaders in their families, in business and in ministry. But above all, "A woman who fears the LORD is to be praised" (Proverbs 31:30).

Lightening the Mother Load: Remember Dr. Mears's words, and allow them to encourage you: "Wherever Christ goes, womanhood is lifted up. . . . In Christian lands, woman is equal to man" (p. 209).

Musings for Moms:
• Read Proverbs 31. Does the description of this woman inspire you or depress you? Why?

• Read Proverbs 2:6. In what ways do you receive wisdom?

• Do you think someone who is wise is also perfect, or do you think you can be perfect without being wise?

Keeping Up with the Joneses

Snapshot from Henrietta: Without God, life is full of disappointment and weariness. Period. Solomon, the author of Proverbs, is also the ascribed author of this book. Solomon went through a period of doubt and questioning with God, something many of us also struggle with. In this book, he asks some pretty deep questions and basically arrives at the conclusion that without God, life is full of disappointment and weariness. Solomon didn't just take someone else's word for this. He tried many different ways to find his happiness apart from God, including philosophy, drinking, building, possessions, wealth, music, and more . . . in other words, he had his challenges, too. But he ultimately came to the conclusion (as hopefully we do, sooner rather than later) that we have a need for God that only He can fill.

Mom Moments with Miss Mears

Her Synopsis:
Jesus Christ, the End of All Living

Her Suggested Bible Readings:
Ecclesiastes 3:1-22   There is a time for everything
Ecclesiastes 11:7-10   Knowing God at a young age
Ecclesiastes 12:13-14   Fearing God

Momento: Keeping up with the Joneses is another name for the comparison trap.

Scripture: "And I saw that all labor and all achievement spring from man's envy of his neighbor. This too is meaningless, a chasing after the wind" (Ecclesiastes 4:4).

MAMA MIA

Every once in a while I get sucked back into the comparison trap or the "keeping up with the Joneses" mentality. I hate when that happens, which is more often than I care to admit.

I suspect you may have had this experience: A friend or neighbor gets something new. Perhaps it's something big like a house, or something in-between like a new car, or even something small like a new outfit. It doesn't really matter what it is, but it's new and better than what you have, and the envy bug bites.

The antidote to the envy bug is gratitude and filling the emptiness not with big, bigger, biggest, but with God, godlier, godliest.

When we first built our home several years ago, I was overwhelmed by the size and newness of it. It was almost twice as big as our first home and easily three times the size of the home we had just moved out of. But over time the newness wore off and our development expanded with newer and larger homes.

What had once been my castle on the hill now felt outdated. The cabinets had scratches on them, the walls had scrapes and marks, the carpet had spots from countless spills, and the white tile on the kitchen floor was impossible to keep clean. (What on earth had ever possessed me to put white tile on the floor anyway?)

Not only were newer homes being erected around us, but also neighbors were having their basements finished, converting them into large areas for added work and play. The last time the envy bug bit me was after I visited a neighbor and toured her new basement. It was absolutely gorgeous, and all of a sudden a huge wave of covetousness and dissatisfaction with my own home swept over me.

My friend's basement was nicer than my entire house! She had a kitchen in her basement, complete with a granite countertop, and stainless steel appliances. There was a family room with a big-screen TV, complete with stadium seating. There was a decorated office that I would be reluctant to work in because it was too perfect, not to mention the craft room stocked with everything AC Moore and Michael's has to offer.

I left feeling dissatisfied and envious, forgetting about how much I did have.

But God reminded me about another friend who was living with her six children in a much smaller house, a house that cost less than my neighbor's basement renovations. He also reminded me that there are many in the world who live in one-room homes with several family members, and it didn't take long to shift my perspective from an attitude of covetousness to one of gratitude.

It is so easy to get sucked back into the consumer mindset of big, bigger, biggest. Just remember that God says this too is meaningless, a chasing after the wind. Let us instead chase after God.

Lightening the Mother Load: Envy and covetousness have a way of creeping into our lives, pulling our focus away from the blessings we do have. Incorporating a daily practice of gratitude helps to make certain that keeping up with the Joneses doesn't overwhelm our keeping up with God.

Musings for Moms:
· How do the words from Ecclesiastes 1:2, "Everything is meaningless," strike you?

· Who or what do you compare yourself to? How does the comparison make you feel?

· Have your kids seen you drooling over something you'd like to have but don't? Is this a behavior you want your kids to copy?

White Teeth and Plastic Surgery

Snapshot from Henrietta: Hey, hold on to your hats. There's some steamy dialogue in this book, written by Solomon, who also penned Proverbs. Didn't know the Bible could wax seductive, as in chick-lit romance reading? Yup, it surprised me too. Song of Solomon contains dialogue between wise King Solomon and a woman from Shulam (also referred to as a Shulamite) that symbolically paints a picture of God's love for His people. It is a wonderful portrait of personal love for Christ, which Dr. Mears calls "the greatest need of the Church today" (p. 217). It's just that the writing is a bit more explicit in this particular book—at least PG-13 and sometimes even R. No wonder it doesn't get much flannel-board attention!

Mom Moments with Miss Mears

Her Synopsis:

Jesus Christ, the Lover of Our Souls

Her Suggested Bible Readings:

Song of Songs 1:1-4   The lover of our souls knows that we are beautiful

Momento: How many women are satisfied with their physical appearance, especially after they have had a child or two? Breasts like a fawn? You're kidding, right?

Scripture: "Your teeth are like a flock of sheep just shorn, coming up from the washing. . . . Your lips are like a scarlet ribbon; your mouth is lovely. . . . Your neck is like the tower of David, built with elegance. . . . Your two breasts are like two fawns, like twin fawns of a gazelle that browse among the lilies" (Song of Songs 4:2-5).

MAMA MIA

I understand that I should love and accept my body just the way it is, but it was much easier to do so years ago when I was in my twenties, before I had birthed three children and succumbed to the effects of gravitational aging, which seemed to be pulling various body parts downward.

Instead of being critical of our bodies and looking to current culture and media (which have access to airbrushes and surgical techniques) for a definition of beauty, we need to view our bodies as God views them. We are His beautiful children whose "body is a temple to the Holy Spirit" (1 Corinthians 6:19).

But God also created a woman's body to be alluring and appealing to her husband. Just read Song of Songs! The descriptions of our beauty are breathtaking. "Song of Songs has been called the Christian's love song" (p. 217).

After giving birth to and raising our children, "alluring" and "appealing" aren't exactly the words that come to mind when I look in the mirror. Stretch marks, leaking or sagging breasts, and an extra 20 pounds may come up in conversation, but "alluring" and "appealing"? And childbirth isn't the only event that takes its toll on our bodies. Middle age (which I am in) has added the complication of decreased metabolism and looming menopause to the picture.

I remember one year asking for liposuction for Christmas. "I just wish I could get rid of 20 pounds between my naval and my knees." Santa didn't bring me liposuction (or Botox for my brow for that matter), just clothes that were the next size up.

What I should have asked for was a new lens through which to view my body.

Our bodies are strong; they are designed to carry and birth children. Our breasts give nourishment to our babies and are alluring to our mate. The curves of our hips accommodate the passage of a baby down the birth canal and also exhibit a softness and roundness that our husband also finds attractive. Our feet carry us through the responsibilities of our day, and our hands can stroke, soothe, caress and be raised in worship.

So take a peek through God's mirror, and then raise your hands in worship to the God who created you in beauty and radiance. "How beautiful you are, my darling! Oh, how beautiful!" (Song of Songs 4:1).

Lightening the Mother Load: God's eyes view us as His beautiful daughters, regardless of our age or size.

Musings for Moms:
- What is the media's idea of physical beauty? Is the idea realistic? How has it hurt society?

- Are you satisfied with your physical appearance? Do you believe God loves you just as you are?

- Do you think today's society and culture set unrealistic standards for physical beauty? Have you ever undergone a cosmetic procedure? If so, did you feel happier afterward?

Past Mistakes

Snapshot from Henrietta: Isaiah is the first of a group of five books referred to as the Major Prophets (Isaiah, Jeremiah, Lamentations, Ezekiel and Daniel). These prophets were handpicked by God to perform the ongoing thankless task of notifying the Israelites of what they were in for if they didn't shape up. The problem the Israelites had was a listening problem . . . well, that was only one of many problems. They were also disobedient, throwing away all morality and religion. Needless to say, the prophets (who were always fearless Israelites) were not the most popular guys on the block. God only called prophets during really bleak times, and this was the beginning of a very long, dark time in Israel's history— 500 years to be exact (which included both the major and minor prophets) spanning the tenth to fifth century BC. Truth and transparency was the name of the game for the prophets, all of whom spoke boldly to both the kings and the people about their sins and failures. Isaiah had the privilege of being God's first mouthpiece, spanning four kings from 739 to 686 BC.

Mom Moments with Miss Mears

Her Synopsis:
Isaiah Portrays Jesus Christ, the Messiah

Her Suggested Bible Readings:

Isaiah 1:1-18	Rebelliousness
Isaiah 9:6-7	The image of God, our hope and Savior
Isaiah 11:1-9	The Spirit of the Lord
Isaiah 40:1-5	Comfort
Isaiah 55:1-3	The thirsty are quenched

Momento: Moms, as imperfect human beings, make their share of mistakes.

Scripture: "Do not be afraid; you will not suffer shame. Do not fear disgrace; you will not be humiliated. You will forget the shame of your youth and remember no more the reproach of your widowhood" (Isaiah 54:4).

MAMA MIA

I have made my share of mistakes, both as a mom and as a child. Does that sound familiar?

I remember with chagrin some of the mistakes I made as a kid, but I take hope and solace in the fact that I "will forget the shame of [my] youth" (Isaiah 54:4). I hope I can also forget the shame of some of the parenting mistakes I have made as a mom—God has had to teach me a lesson or two.

Sometimes I have a hard time remembering that as a parent, my job is not to win popularity contests with my kids. Thankfully, I am always popular in God's eyes, even though I don't always get my way! Like a reasonable and prudent parent, God doesn't always say yes and often disciplines me as well. Yet He still loves me and will forget the mistakes I make. That's a great parenting model. Now if only I could keep it front and center!

Sometimes I succumb to pressure from my kids to get them the latest gadget. I am particularly vulnerable to making a mistake if I am distracted and don't stay focused on God or the priorities in my life. It doesn't really matter what the identified object of desire is . . . I venture to say we have all lived some version of the following parental error. See if you can relate.

The most recent object of my daughter's desire was an iPod Touch—the latest and greatest in songs, video, games and endless entertainment . . . and wireless for anyone (including me), if we happened to be in a wireless hot spot. (I sheepishly admit she was nine. What was I thinking?)

Nicole didn't have enough money to purchase it herself, and her birthday wasn't for a couple of months. I reasoned that the cost of the iPod Touch was similar to what we had spent on past parties, so I offered her an alternative.

"Hey, Nicole, you can choose which you would rather have: an iPod Touch or a birthday party." I was correct in assuming she would choose the gadget to the gathering. What I hadn't counted on was her adept and persistent coaxing of said item far ahead of her actual birthday, which was not until May. Guilt and gullibility were weaknesses she correctly identified and focused on in her bid to coax the item out of me—sooner rather than later!

Several life events had recently conspired to make me particularly vulnerable to taking the path of least resistance, which included walking into the Apple store and purchasing the iPod Touch for my daughter an entire two months prior to her birthday.

How did this happen?

"Mom, we're right here. There isn't an Apple store anywhere near where we live" (a true statement—we live in the middle of nowhere).

"Mom, you are so busy. This will keep me entertained" (but only after hours of loading the entertainment onto the device).

"Mom, you are the best" (it is not our job to be our kids' friend—we must not abandon reason to flattery that is self-serving).

I fell for her persuasive arguments and gushing kindness hook, line and sinker. Unfortunately they were short-lived, and buyer's remorse set in. This was in large part due to the fact that her personality changed from skillful and charming negotiator to ungrateful and frustrated child. What had I done? How had I been bamboozled into this decision? How could I not hang my head in shame over this mistake? And, more importantly, I thought, *Now what?*

I took the stand I should have and the one that would have been far more effective (and the one that falls into the recommended "do as I say and not as I do" category) had I simply done the correct thing in the first place. I took the electronic device back to the store—despite arguments, fits and other red-headed strong-willed unsavory behavior—and followed through with its return.

Yes, I had blown the initial opportunity for several lessons on how things work in the real world, as well as lessons about our relationship with God. But God uses our mistakes to teach us, and His truth will prevail.

Parents can and do make mistakes. Don't be afraid. Allow yourself to move past your mistakes as God does, and eliminate shame from the mix.

Lightening the Mother Load: Children are not the only ones who make mistakes; moms do too. Thankfully, we always have the opportunity to learn from our mistakes.

Musings for Moms:
· Think about a mistake you have made. Does it still shame you?

· How do you have a conversation with your child about doing as you say but not as you did?

· Read Isaiah 40:29-31. What are your thoughts? What are God's promises to you in these verses? In light of these verses, how do you feel about mistakes you have made?

Words like Arrows

Snapshot from Henrietta: Jeremiah is the second of the Major Prophets, and his audience didn't like his message any more than Isaiah's did. As a matter of fact, they were even less receptive. Poor Jeremiah, he was just minding his own business in his small, out-of-the-way town when God called him to be His prophet during one of the bleakest times in Israel's history. Israel had been taken into captivity, and Judah was in a bad state. But God encouraged him, telling him, "Do not be afraid of them, for I am with you and will rescue you" (Jeremiah 1:7-8). It's a good thing, too, because as I said, Jeremiah's message wasn't any more popular than Isaiah's. And it didn't get better; in fact Dr. Mears notes that "Jeremiah's life was one of deepening gloom" (p. 253).

Mom Moments with Miss Mears

Her Synopsis:
Jeremiah Portrays Jesus Christ, the Righteous Branch

Her Suggested Bible Readings:

Jeremiah 1:1-10	Moms as God's mouthpiece
Jeremiah 9:1-16	The tongue can be trouble!
Jeremiah 23:23-24, 30-32	God is everywhere and knows the truth

Momento: Mothers need to choose their words carefully when speaking to their kids. How many moms have been guilty of sharp and unkind words with their kids?

Scripture: "Their tongue is a deadly arrow; it speaks with deceit. With his mouth each speaks cordially to his neighbor, but in his heart he sets a trap for him" (Jeremiah 9:8).

MAMA MIA

God instructs us to speak "the truth in love" (Ephesians 4:15). But sometimes the words that slip out of my mouth are anything but loving, or the tone is more sarcastic than it is sacramental.

The old saying "Sticks and stones may break your bones but words will never hurt you" is, unfortunately, false. Words can and do inflict tremendous pain. We would do well as moms (in all areas of life, really) to communicate the fruit of the spirit: "love, joy, peace, patience, kindness, goodness, faithfulness, gentleness and self-control" (Galatians 5:23) when we speak. But sometimes our tongue does become a deadly arrow, and we don't communicate kindly.

We all have said things we wish we could snatch back. The words from Ephesians 4:29 are worth heeding: "Do not let any unwholesome talk come out of your mouths, but only what is helpful for building others up according to their needs, that it may benefit those who listen." But, then again, we all fall short of the glory of God and make mistakes.

There have been times my words have been caustic rather than caring; my remarks pointed rather than pure; the tone of my voice harsh with an edge sharp enough to cut through diamonds. The wounds to my children because the voice was mine or because the comments came from my lips have created lasting memories for them blanketed in hurt.

But there are ways to take the sting out of the arrow, even if it flies out of your mouth before you can stop it, and all those ways are expressions of God's grace and humility: apologize. Hug. Make eye contact. Tell your child you love him or her and promise to try harder the next time not to allow the arrow to launch.

Admit that you too make mistakes but yearn to learn from God who does not. And receive and accept the gift of new beginnings that God graciously gives.

Lightening the Mother Load: Sometimes, perhaps more often than we realize, it is best to remain silent. If in doubt, say nothing.

Musings for Moms:

· Has there been a time when words inflicted a wound deeper than any physical injury you have sustained?

· How often do you say things you wish you hadn't? What might help you hold your tongue?

· What does "speaking the truth in love" mean?

One Day at a Time

Snapshot from Henrietta: The book of Lamentations is attributed to Jeremiah and is a continuation of the sorrowful tale of God's people. This time, though, it is written in poetic format and includes five loud cries. As Dr. Mears points out, though, the book "is not all sorrow. Above the clouds of the poet's weeping over the sins of his people, God's sun is shining" (p. 255). But it was still a bleak time. The Babylonian king, Nebuchadnezzar, and his cronies had destroyed Jerusalem.

I love the imagery of rays of sunshine. God still sends us the message of hope through rays of sunshine that break through the clouds. When I see isolated sunbeams streaming down through a patch of clouds, I feel as if God is reaching down and touching me with His grace and hope. It is worth remembering that we can extend that same source of compassion to others.

Mom Moments with Miss Mears

Her Synopsis:
Lamentations Portrays Jesus Christ, the Righteous Branch

Her Suggested Bible Readings:
Lamentations 3:22-23   Compassion that never fails
Lamentations 3:40-66   God's limitless love

Momento: Ask any mom of a prodigal child how she got through the sorrow and grief she experienced, and somewhere in the answer is most likely a version of "one day at a time."

Scripture: "Because of the LORD's great love we are not consumed, for his compassions never fail. They are new every morning; great is your faithfulness" (Lamentations 3:22-25).

MAMA MIA

Parenting has challenges at every step. And as much as we love our children, we need God's grace, hope and love to fuel us to skillfully bring our children through each stage of their development.

Infants challenge moms in the sleep department.

Toddlers challenge moms in the no and why department.

School-age kids challenge moms in their ability to remember third-grade math.

Tweens challenge moms with social drama.

Teens challenge moms (and dads, of course) with rebellion. Why don't the parenting classes give us a hint about the teenage years ahead? Parents may need an extra dose of compassion, love and faithfulness during this stage.

Sometimes parents negotiate the teen years without unreasonable rebellion, but then the kids still have an opportunity to rebel as young adults. No matter what the stage, there are challenges; it just seems that the rebellious years bring pain in need of extra grace.

We cruised through the early and mid-teen years with our older son without a ripple. But when our younger son was about to turn 16, it was as if an earthquake that had been dormant for years hit our household. Everyone was caught in the rubble—and there were several aftershocks. When our second son was just about to turn 16, he discovered marijuana.

I needed help; I needed to talk to another mom who had gone through the same heartache, but I couldn't find one willing to share. I thought I was losing my mind, and I felt alone. I knew there were other moms out there with a similar problem, but where were they? How were they getting through this?

I needed compassion and comfort. I needed God—His compassion and a fresh start every day—but didn't know how to find Him. But He knew how to find me. The theology of self-sufficiency that I had been brought up on had let me down. But God was there, waiting for me to rest in Him.

Through a series of events too remarkable to be coincidental, I went to church with a friend, and there I met the God of hope, compassion and new beginnings. I would love to say all the hurt, heartache and chaos went away overnight, but it didn't. But what did change was my belief that somehow we would get through this as long as we took it one step at a time. Sometimes the hope was hidden by the dark clouds of despair, but it was always there.

It is difficult to hold on to hope when things appear bleak, but the rays of hope that are hidden behind the clouds of sorrow will eventually break through. Beams of light sent directly from God will touch and heal us. God will comfort us.

Lightening the Mother Load: Allow the beams of light God sends you to illuminate your way, and then share that light with others.

Musings for Moms:
- What factors influence your willingness to share your sorrows with others?

- Why do you believe God allows times of sorrow?

- How are you able to extend a hand of hope and healing to parents of prodigals?

What's One More?

Snapshot from Henrietta: Ezekiel, the next of God's chosen prophets, found himself in Babylon along with a whole group of Israelites kicked out of Jerusalem. As such, he became the first prophet to the exiles. As Dr. Mears reminds us, "We must get alongside people to help them" (p. 260). Who better understands pain or sorrow than someone who has had the same experience? Ezekiel was one of them—a captive ministering to captives—and ministered to the exiles as both a prophet and as a priest. In both roles, he proclaimed God's sovereignty and shepherded the exiled flock with a message of hope.

Mom Moments with Miss Mears

Her Synopsis:
Ezekiel Portrays Jesus Christ, the Son of Man

Her Suggested Bible Readings:

Ezekiel 28:25-26	God's promise
Ezekiel 34:11-31	Tending the flock
Ezekiel 37:1-14	Valley of dry bones

Momento: Each neighborhood has a shepherd mom, one who takes care of the flock. Never underestimate the impact that simple acts of kindness can have.

Scripture: "Son of man, prophesy against the shepherds of Israel; prophesy and say to them: 'This is what the Sovereign LORD says: Woe to the shepherds of Israel who only take care of themselves! Should not shepherds take care of the flock?'" (Ezekiel 34:2).

MAMA MIA

My girls are social creatures, always wanting to have a friend over. Sometimes it is for an after-school play date, sometimes for a sleepover and sometimes for an impromptu party.

I love hosting these events. I love being the den mother who has kids coming and going. In many ways, I find kids easier to have over than adults! After all, kids don't care whether your house is a mess, they will eat anything (and everything), they generally get along, and you don't need to entertain them. Sometimes it's chaotic, but it is always fun. You don't really need to have a special occasion to have some friends over, just an open heart and an open home. And my girls know their friends are always welcome.

Recently, my daughters asked if they could invite a group of friends over for an ice-cream-sundae party. The girls sat down and created invitations on the computer and put together a shopping list and then burst with excitement.

Party day arrived, and we had a wonderful bonus in that the weather was nice and that the group of kids could play outside. Inside would have been a bit more challenging, but the kids still would have had fun. Sometimes the neat freak in me becomes challenged, but I remind myself of the importance of people to Jesus—more important than what the house looks like or what food is served (read the story of Martha and Mary in Luke 10:38-42).

The ice-cream-sundae party turned out to be a model of true hospitality. A few friends gathered, some food was shared, and the group created a community of fellowship. My girls served the ice cream, invited the friends to play, and even cleaned up the mess, which earned them the opportunity to do it again.

Jesus loves that sort of hospitality. Think about the number of meals and social gatherings He attended! He provides the model. Nothing fancy required.

So the next time you have an opportunity to be the neighborhood mom, think of it as honoring God.

Lightening the Mother Load: Hospitality is one way we can share love with others—both our own and God's.

Musings for Moms:

• Do you prefer to have kids over to your house, or have your child hang out somewhere else with their friends? Why?

• What kind of mom do your kids consider you to be? Do you enjoy being the "den mom" to a flock of kids? Do you volunteer to chaperone class trips or help out at Sunday School?

• What kinds of things can you do or what kinds of roles can you assume to improve your "shepherding" skills?

Holding Fast to Faith

Snapshot from Henrietta: While Ezekiel was prophesying to the Israelites held captive in Babylon, his contemporary, Daniel, was prophesying there as well; only his audience was different. He found himself smack dab in King Nebuchadnezzar's palace. So he might have had the cushy physical surroundings, but his audience was hostile and foreign. At least Ezekiel was talking to fellow Israelites—not so for Daniel. But Daniel obeyed God and was appointed prime minister of Babylon. Go figure—another God thing. And there are plenty of God things in this book, many of which get Sunday School flannel-board attention, like the story of Daniel in the lions' den (chapter 6) and the story of Daniel's buddies Shadrach, Meshach and Abednego (chapter 3).

Mom Moments with Miss Mears

Her Synopsis:
Daniel Portrays Jesus Christ, the Striking Stone

Her Suggested Bible Readings:

Daniel 3:1-30   The fiery furnace
Daniel 6:1-28   The lions' den

Momento: Staying true to our faith can be really tough in the face of adversity.

Scripture: "If we are thrown into the blazing furnace, the God we serve is able to save us from it, and he will rescue us from your hand, O king. But even if he does not, we want you to know, O king, that we will not serve your gods or worship the image of gold you have set up" (Daniel 3:17-18).

MAMA MIA

Sometimes life is hard. Very hard. But God is there to help carry the load, so don't be afraid to collapse into His loving arms if you are weary.

I have always loved the story told in "Footprints in the Sand." Most of us are familiar with this poem, which has made its way onto numerous plaques and various gift items. If you are not familiar with it, the poem is basically about two sets of footprints in the sand, one for a person who is dreaming about a walk with God, and one for the Lord. As the dreamer looks back on his life, he notices that at times there was only one set of footprints. When the dreamer questions why, the Lord answers, "During your times of trial and suffering, when you see only one set of footprints, it was then that I carried you."

One night, just two weeks before he died, my dad gave me a post-card with this poem on it. It was as if he knew I was the one who would need to be carried just a short time later. It was a gift of grace to me from God through my dad. We enjoyed a beyond-wonderful evening together that night. The last words I ever said to my dad were, "I love you."

We know that there will be tough times in life. Jesus tells us so in God's Word: "I have told you these things, so that in me you may have peace. In this world you will have trouble. But take heart! I have overcome the world" (John 16:33).

A time of trouble may not always involve a death; it may involve some other sort of catastrophic event, or it may simply be a series of annoyances. A time of trouble is any event or experience that aims or conspires to distract us from serving God and loving our families. Regardless, know that you don't have to carry the burden of adversity yourself. No matter whether the outcome is what you desire or not, God will meet you in that place and carry you when the journey becomes too difficult.

Allow yourself to be carried.

Lightening the Mother Load: Some days you may feel like you are hanging on to life by a string; know and believe God is holding on to the other end and will never let go.

Musings for Moms:

· Have there been times you have been angry with God? When?

· Read the story of Daniel in the lions' den in chapter 6. Have you ever been in a seemingly impossible situation where God intervened and rescued you?

· Have you ever found yourself in your own "fiery furnace"? Do you believe the promise that God will never leave you or forsake you?

Gomer Is Not a Goner

Snapshot from Henrietta: Hosea is the first of the next 12 books of the Bible that are collectively known as the Minor Prophets. This doesn't mean that their message was any less important than the prophets who had come before; rather, it simply means that they had shorter messages. Hosea is another great love story, symbolic of Jehovah's love for Israel (encountered before in the Song of Songs). In this book, the story is about Hosea and his unwavering devotion to his adulterous wife, Gomer.

Mom Moments with Miss Mears

Her Synopsis:
Jesus Christ, Healer of the Backslider

Her Suggested Bible Readings:
Hosea 3:1-4   Reconciliation

Momento: Obedience is more important than appearance.

Scripture: "When the LORD began to speak through Hosea, the LORD said to him, 'Go take to yourself an adulterous wife and children of unfaithfulness, because the land is guilty of the vilest adultery in departing from the LORD.' So he married Gomer daughter of Diblaim, and she conceived and bore him a son" (Hosea 1:2-3).

MAMA MIA

I feel for Hosea. He was called to not only prophesy a message the Jews didn't want to hear, but he was also asked to live that message in his life. The Jews were still being unfaithful to God and wouldn't obey Him, so God asked Hosea to marry an unfaithful wife and love her tenderly despite her adulterous digressions.

Dr. Mears describes Hosea as "one of the greatest lovers in all literature. We find his love so strong that even the worst actions of an unfaithful wife could not kill it" (p. 292). She goes on to write, "Gomer ran away from home and left her young husband. . . . Lured away by the sin about her, she fell into the moral cesspool of the day and finally was carried off as a slave. Through it all, Hosea was true to her. Still loving her, he tried everything to win her back to a happy family life. But she would not" (p. 293).

I wonder what Hosea's parents (and friends) had to say about Gomer. I can just hear his mom saying, "Hosea, what are you thinking marrying a girl like that? She isn't good enough for you." But Hosea loved Gomer, and the only voice he listened to was God's. He was willing to sacrifice what other people thought of him in order to please and obey God. Despite all the heartbreak, Hosea hung in there. He loved Gomer long after she left him for someone else, and he continued to raise their children, always proclaiming his love for her.

This same story plays out in today's world over and over again. Perhaps you know couples who are unequally yoked. Even though the marriage may end (sometimes in divorce, but not always), one partner resolutely and steadfastly continues to love. Instead of focusing on the betrayal, think about the love and commitment. Wouldn't it be wonderful to be the object of that kind of intense love?

That's the kind of love God has for us. Even if we leave Him (repeatedly), He still longs for us to fall back into His arms. We can disappoint Him, feel like we aren't good enough and even be told we're not good enough, yet He waits for us with open arms.

Human love may fail, but God's love never will.

Lightening the Mother Load: There is no better gift than enduring love, the kind of love we receive from God. May we pass it
along to others.

Musings for Moms:

· Does a woman's reputation matter when a man is choosing a
wife? Do you think a woman's reputation affects what kind of
mother she is or will become?

· Have you ever loved someone who didn't return your love? How
did you feel about the situation?

· What are the people asked to do in Hosea 14? What is the re-
sultant promise?

Don't Be Afraid to Ask for Help!

Snapshot from Henrietta: Warning, warning, warning . . . judgment, judgment, judgment . . . and locusts, locusts, locusts. This book has plenty of all three. I love this verse from Joel: "I will repay you for the years the locusts have eaten" (Joel 2:25). I love it because of the promise of hope it conveys. You know all those years you lost to sorrow and heartache? Well, guess what? Jehovah God will restore them to you! I hold on to that promise!

Hosea was a prophet to Israel, and Joel was a prophet to Judah. Joel kept trying to warn the people, but they didn't get it; it just didn't sink in. In the three short chapters of this book, Joel uses the phrase "the day of the Lord" five times. The day of the Lord referred to the day of God's judgment, which was inevitable.

There's another great promise in this short book: "I will pour out my Spirit on all people. . . . Even on my servants, both men and women, . . . and everyone who calls on the name of the LORD will be saved" (Joel 2:28-29,32). God's spirit isn't solely reserved for the Jewish people but for everyone—women (moms) included. Wow!

Mom Moments with Miss Mears

Her Synopsis:
Jesus Christ, Restorer

Her Suggested Bible Readings:

Joel 2:12-13	Return to God
Joel 2:32	Call on God's name
Joel 3:17-21	Restoration

Momento: Like our kids, we can get into messy situations. But there is a solution. Rather than respond with pride and refuse to ask for help, we can get some guidance, both from others and from God.

Scripture: "And everyone who calls on the name of the LORD will be saved" (Joel 2:32).

MAMA MIA

Every once in a while, parenting throws us moms a curve ball. Instead of hitting it foul, try to make it a home run. Of course, hitting home runs requires practice—and often some coaching too. Fortunately, we have a coaching staff to whom we can turn.

Moms have lots of outside resources they can turn to for help. There is a plethora of parenting classes, books, websites and support groups available, and, when needed, moms can get professional advice. If you are overwhelmed, don't be afraid to turn to others (counselors and educational consultants, to name just two) for help.

Of course, it is also crucial to remember to turn to God, our head coach, through the help of the Counselor (the Holy Spirit), who functions much like a team manager, having several alternatives in the wings to ensure the best outcome. He is always available with an alternative game plan depending on the opponent. All His help is free, a benefit of playing on God's team.

One day, I did reach my breaking point, and after much prayer and consideration, I finally made a call to a Christian counselor whose number I had stashed away in my wallet for weeks. Nicole was screaming in the background, and I couldn't hear myself think, let alone hear the voice on the other end of the phone. It was the perfect "description" of the help I needed.

"Don't call . . . don't call! You don't need to call!" she hollered at the top of her lungs. She then made a move to click the receiver and end my conversation. I took the phone with me into "my office" (the bathroom) and leaned against the door to prevent her from following me. The voice on the other end of the line acknowledged that it sounded like we needed help and scheduled an appointment.

We engaged the help of this Christian counselor, who included prayer and spiritual direction as part of the therapeutic healing process. Along with God and the Holy Spirit, this counselor was part of our coaching team.

Don't be afraid to sign up for some coaching if you start to hit too many foul balls. There is a team out there waiting to help you hit home runs.

Lightening the Mother Load: God is our head coach and available 24/7. Call Him first.

Musings for Moms:

• How is God described in Joel 2:13? Do these words describe how you view God? If not, what words do?

• Read Joel 2:25. Does this verse fill you with hope? What time in your life was a time that "the locusts ate"?

• Read Joel 2:28-32. Put the promises written in these verses into your own words.

Hide-and-Seek

Snapshot from Henrietta: Amos was another shepherd called by God. (Remember King David?) Well, here's Amos, minding his own business, and God calls him to try to set the people straight. During Amos's day there was great prosperity both in Israel and in Judah down south. God's people were just having too much darn fun—buying the latest and greatest and rejecting God at every turn—and Amos couldn't get their attention. Lavish spending and military victories were the norm. Who needed God? It seemed preposterous that God's Chosen People would experience anything but continued successes. God would never hide His face from them. But less than 50 years later, Israel was destroyed. Too bad they didn't listen when Amos tried to tell them how to find God.

Mom Moments with Miss Mears

Her Synopsis:
Jesus Christ, Heavenly Husbandman

Her Suggested Bible Readings:
Amos 4:6-12   God's discipline
Amos 9:2-4   You can't hide from God

Momento: Sooner or later, truth catches up with us.

Scripture: "Though they hide themselves on the top of Carmel, there I will hunt them down and seize them. Though they hide from me at the bottom of the sea, there I will command the serpent to bite them" (Amos 9:3).

MAMA MIA

Running away and hiding is nothing new. There are times we run from God and His truth, and there are times we run away from people or situations where we know we have been wrong. Regardless of how far or fast we run, however, sooner or later we are found. The key is to recognize our mistakes, ask for forgiveness and move forward.

I have a powerful childhood memory that I have carried with me into adulthood. I had made a mistake, and I had tried to run and hide. However, hiding hadn't worked then, and I need to remember that it won't work now that I am an adult, either.

My dad, an artist, had a wooden model of a hand with moveable fingers that he used in his studio whenever he needed to draw hands. The hand could be positioned into a variety of poses, fingers gracefully extended or cupped to hold an object. Often there would be rings on the fingers or the hand would be holding a flower.

I enjoyed changing the position of the hand and picked it up one day to move the fingers around. I bent the fingers back and forth, experimenting with what it must be like to be double-jointed, when the tip of the index finger broke off in my hand.

I panicked and didn't know what to do. So I did what any reasonable seven-year-old (or so) would do. I picked up the broken hand and hid it. I stuffed it inside a pillowcase and then shoved it under some covers on the guest bed. Then I went to play with my Barbies, hoping my dad wouldn't notice the hand was missing.

But he did.

"Kathy!" I heard my name being called in a tone that meant business. The same hands that had caused the broken fingertip and then had tried to hide all the evidence started to shake.

"What?" I answered, trying to prevent my voice from squeaking.

"Do you know where my wooden hand is?"

"What hand?" I asked. I abandoned my Barbies and scrambled to take cover. I crawled underneath a table with a tablecloth that concealed me perfectly. I hid there the entire time both my parents searched high and low (for me and the hand, I suspect); the tone in their voice communicating their disappointment and frustration.

I imagine Amos heard the same tone of voice from God when the Israelites were trying to hide from him.

My plan for concealment ultimately didn't work, and not too much more time elapsed before my dad finally lifted up the table-cloth and discovered me cowering under the table. My lying and my location had both been discovered.

"Young lady, come out from underneath there!" he commanded. The fact that I had been addressed as "young lady" wasn't very promising.

I had been discovered, and it was time to suffer the consequences of my poor choices. Not only had I hidden, but I had also lied. I can still remember this event as if it had happened yesterday.

I *did* learn a valuable lesson, though: Lying and hiding, whether from God or others, doesn't work. And, like God, my parents searched for me until they found me; they wanted me to recognize my mistake just as God wants us to absorb that same truth when we run from Him.

God's love is relentless, and even when we make mistakes and try to hide, He will search for us to bring us back into His family.

Lightening the Mother Load: In the game of hide-and-seek, God always wins. Ultimately it is impossible to out-hide God.

Musings for Moms:
· What does God promise us if we follow His command in Amos 5:14?

· Have your kids ever lied to you? If so, did they try to conceal their deceit? How can you teach them to trust you with the truth?

· Have there been times you have tried to hide from God? Do you think it is possible to hide from God? Can such attempts be used as a teaching tool?

Tit for Tat

Snapshot from Henrietta: This book is direct and to the point. The shortest book in the Bible, it carries a simple message: Bullies beware! Proud and rebellious rebel rousers are doomed, while those who are humble and meek will make it. We hear again about "the day of the Lord," but this time the destruction refers to the Edomites. Obadiah's warning is clear: If you don't knock it off (picking on His people), "there will be no survivors" (Obadiah 18).

Mom Moments with Miss Mears

Her Synopsis:
Jesus Christ, Our Savior

Her Suggested Bible Readings:
Obadiah 1-21   Selfishness will not prevail

Momento: Leave scorekeeping up to God. (This is a message I need to remind myself of often.)

Scripture: "The day of the LORD is near for all nations. As you have done, it will be done to you; your deeds will return upon your own head" (Obadiah 15).

MAMA MIA

"As you have done, it will be done to you" is the biblical version of the common phrase "what goes around comes around." So why do we sometimes feel such a need to keep score?

Everyday events give us plenty of opportunities to either keep score or bless others through humble and generous giving with nothing expected in return. "God loves a cheerful giver," Paul writes in 2 Corinthians 9:7, but giving cheerfully, especially if we feel like the person we are giving to doesn't deserve it, sometimes takes a conscious effort that escapes many of us.

I don't know about you, but I used to have a hard time not keeping a mental scorecard of returning favors. Whether it concerned Christmas cards, who paid for the last dinner out, making sure invitations were reciprocated, or the cost of exchanged gifts, the tit-for-tat mentality—which was as ingrained in my human nature as it was in the Edomites—took over.

Not too long ago, I was in my kitchen putting together a gift for a friend, and my girls were helping me.

"Hey, that's a pretty nice gift, Mom," my older daughter, Tianna, commented, taking stock of what I was putting into the basket.

There was a book, candles, a pen and paper, some note cards and several other hot-pink items. The diva in me had gone wild, and it was fun! I was getting carried away finding more and more items to make this gift special.

My friend had been going through a rough stretch, and this was a surprise pick-me-up gift to put a smile on her face.

"Hey, Mom," my other daughter asked, "did she ever send you a gift like that?"

"No," I answered truthfully. I paused and then continued, "But it doesn't matter. I wanted to do something nice for her."

"Well, maybe sometime she'll surprise you," Tianna added, still examining the goodies that made up the basket.

"She might," I answered. Then I added truthfully, "But it's fine if she doesn't."

Over time, God had changed my scorekeeping heart, gently leading me to give more generously from a place inside of me that yearned to bless others. And the funny thing was, I was always delighted and surprised (blessed) by a return act of generosity, which in turn motivated me to share even more.

"You know," I said, speaking to both of my girls, "why don't you think of someone you would like to surprise for no reason and make a goody bag for them."

"Really?" they said in unison. "Just for no reason?" they asked again, making sure they had heard me correctly. They remembered my scorekeeping days well.

"That's right, for no reason except to surprise them." I smiled and looked at them with a twinkle in my eye, and they knew I was serious.

We spent the next hour gathering two more goody bags for friends they thought would enjoy the surprise gifts. We talked about giving generously and not out of a sense of obligation. Jesus never gave out of obligation; He gave from a position of grace. Grace leaves no room for scorekeeping, or tit-for-tat behavior.

The next time you may be tempted to keep score, release the scorecard to God. Allow Him to extend His gifts and grace through you. And let go of the burden of keeping score. Leave that up to God.

Lightening the Mother Load: God values generosity and humility, and He delights in you when you share with others.

Musings for Moms:
- Obadiah 12 tells us to "not look down on [our] brother." Have you ever looked down on another mom?

- In what ways have you kept score?

- Are there times you feel obligated to return an invitation or give someone a gift only because the other person has done so first to you? What kind of message does this send to your kids?

Run, Run as Fast as You Can

Snapshot from Henrietta: Most of us are familiar with Jonah as the guy who was swallowed up by the great big fish (it was a fish, not a whale). But I bet you didn't know that Jonah was a great statesman and had an influential role in bringing the Northern Kingdom of Israel to power and prosperity. But the first time God asked him to be a prophet, Jonah turned Him down.

Bad move. Enter a big fish. When the big fish up-chucked Jonah, he finally agreed—though none too happily—to do what God wanted. He still didn't think the people God wanted to save should be saved. A bit judgmental perhaps? Sure, but God finally got through to him.

Jonah is not only a great story but also an important book of the Bible. "Jonah is the test book of the Bible. It challenges our faith. Our attitude toward Jonah reveals our attitude toward God and His Word" (p. 314).

Mom Moments with Miss Mears

Her Synopsis:
Jesus Christ, Our Resurrection and Life

Her Suggested Bible Readings:

Jonah 1–2	The story of the fish
Jonah 3–4	Obedience

Momento: Running away from our problems will never solve them, so why is it usually our first choice?

Scripture: "But Jonah ran away from the LORD and headed for Tarshish. He went down to Joppa, where he found a ship bound for that port. After paying the fare, he went aboard and sailed for Tarshish to flee from the LORD" (Jonah 1:3).

MAMA MIA

I know I'm not alone in wanting to run away sometimes. There are times when I am living life so on the edge, trying not to fall off, that I sometimes wonder if falling off into a hole (or a fish belly) wouldn't solve things for a while. Have you ever felt that way? Overwhelmed to the point of just running away? Why is it we choose to run away from God rather than right into His waiting arms?

I know I'm not the only one. My friend Connie, a breast-cancer survivor, felt the same way when she was undergoing treatment several years ago.

"I just wanted to go home," Connie started her story, remembering how she desperately wanted to leave her family and run away to her parent's home in California. "My house was littered with dirty dishes, the Sunday newspaper lay scattered across the dining room table (it was Wednesday), and piles of clean clothes lay in clumps on the sofa—unfolded. I remember slumping down in the easy chair, which wasn't making my life any easier, with my head in my hands just overcome with the feeling that I wanted to go home." Connie paused and then added, "I desperately wanted to flee and never return."

"Couldn't someone manage to put the milk back in the refrigerator?" she sighed as she continued to tell me about the mess from the night before that greeted her when she had returned home from a treatment appointment. "Then I took a sniff of the open container and barely made it to the bathroom before the contents of my lunch spewed out." Her expression told me that even though what she described had occurred over 10 years ago, the memory was still fresh.

Connie continued, "I grabbed onto the toilet bowl as if I was hanging on for my life and waited for the wave of nausea to pass. If I was in my twenties, I could chalk it up to morning sickness, but not now at 40. How I wish it was morning sickness."

It had been a very difficult time in my friend's life. This sickness was different; the side effects of treatment for breast cancer held her in their painful grip. She worked full-time through surgery, treatment and radiation, and she had nothing left to give. She was tired, fearful and angry.

"You know," she said, "moms aren't supposed to get sick. They need to take care of everyone else's needs and keep going . . . no matter what! But I was tired of 'running'; I needed to face my anger of why me, why now? I was 40 years old and in the best shape of my life, yet my body still betrayed me." She shook her head, remembering this difficult period in her life.

She expressed her anger at being young and in great shape; anger as she contemplated her boys' future without a mom; anger that it was her; anger that God had allowed it.

"I remember feeling so lost and confused; and I went upstairs and uttered a simple heartfelt prayer, 'God, I can't be angry anymore. I don't know why this happened, but I need to trust You for the future. I can't run away from my disease, and I can't run away from Your hope. I will stay here and lean on You to bring me through.'"

Connie sighed again, thankful that she had not run away from home but instead had allowed God to bring her through this difficult time.

Lightening the Mother Load: Run toward God, not away from Him; He is there to embrace you.

Musings for Moms:
· What happened the last time you tried to run away from a problem?

· What kind of example do you set for your kids as a problem solver?

· Jonah 4 describes how angry Jonah became with God's compassion. How often do you become angry when someone else gets a break that you feel is undeserved?

God's Requirements

Snapshot from Henrietta: Micah was an ordinary guy and served as a prophet to the common people in the countryside. He tried to tell them that just acting and looking religious wasn't going to cut it, but they really thought that if they looked and acted religious, God wouldn't zap them. (There are still plenty of Christians who believe the same thing.) Micah tells us what God requires of us: "To act justly and to love mercy and to walk humbly with your God" (Micah 6:8). Israel didn't listen, so the people were hauled off into captivity in Babylon; Judah didn't do much better, although you'd think they'd have learned a thing or two. One hundred and fifty years later, they were captured as well.

Mom Moments with Miss Mears

Her Synopsis:
Jesus Christ, Witness Against Rebellious Nations

Her Suggested Bible Readings:
Micah 2:1-13	God's plans or man's plans
Micah 6:8	Our marching orders
Micah 7:7,14-20	Prayer and praise

Momento: Compassion, humility and sharing are all part of being just and serving God.

Scripture: "And what does the LORD require of you? To act justly and to love mercy and to walk humbly with your God" (Micah 6:8).

MAMA MIA

"Done!" I proclaimed, satisfied that I had crammed the last piece of clothing into the final suitcase, which I had to sit on top of to close.

I had managed to pack 10 garbage bags full of clothing into four suitcases to take to Honduras on an upcoming trip. Each bag was loaded to its 50-pound capacity, and I was satisfied that I couldn't stuff another item into the bags. My mom and I would each take our things in carry-ons, using the checked baggage allowance for the bags of donated clothing.

I had been to Honduras before with the girls, who had had a first-hand opportunity to witness poverty and play with children who only owned one or two sets of clothing. And even though they admired the clothes that went into the suitcases and wanted to claim a shirt or two for themselves, they remembered the children they had met and knew these clothes were for them.

For this trip, we had been given a beautiful collection of clothes, many of them new or only gently used. We wanted to honor those to whom we were giving these things to; to view them as special children of God and not as beggars in need of a handout. (I remembered with sadness one trip where the donated clothing and shoes had been worn out and tattered.)

"Hey, Nicole, remember the girl you played with in Honduras? Wasn't her name Maria? Do you remember how she wore the same thing every day? I think she only had one set of clothes, and didn't have any shoes."

"Yeah, I remember," Nicole answered, and slowly her expression started to change. "I remember Maria . . ."

Maria had come to play with Nicole at the nutrition center every day. She was about the same age but weighed 20 pounds less, had stringy hair and had bare feet, which were a tone darker than the rest of her body from a permanent layer of dirt.

Nicole, forgetting about the T-shirt that she had hoped to keep for herself, got up and went into the garage and came back with her favorite pair of sandals and carefully placed them on top of the suitcase.

"Mom, do you think you can find room for these in the suitcase?" she asked. "I want you to take these too and give them to another little girl who doesn't have any shoes."

"I would love that," I answered, making room for them in a side pocket. "And I will tell the girl I give them to that they're from my little girl."

I smiled as the message of sharing and giving to those who have less registered on Nicole's face. And I imagined that God smiled too.

Lightening the Mother Load: Giving and sharing, although sometimes difficult and not our first inclination, always put a smile on God's face and open the door to blessings for everyone.

Musings for Moms:
- Do you know any people who look and act religious, but don't live consistently with their projected image? What impression of Christianity do you think those people give to others?

- How can you make justice and mercy an everyday part of parenting?

- What does "walk humbly" mean? How can you teach your children to do this?

Out of Control

Snapshot from Henrietta: This book brings us back to Ninevah, Assyria's capitol, the same place Jonah went. Only 150 years later, the Ninevites needed a repeat visit from a prophet, this time Nahum. But unlike Jonah, Nahum wasn't sent to warn them to repent. They had blown that opportunity. Rather, Nahum was there to announce their destruction—an absolute, final and certain doom. No more warnings, no more second chances. Wickedness and rebellion led directly to destruction.

Mom Moments with Miss Mears

Her Synopsis:
Jesus Christ, a Stronghold in the Day of Trouble

Her Suggested Bible Readings:
Nahum 1:1-15   A jealous and good God

Momento: Tough love isn't only hard on kids; it's tough on parents too.

Scripture: "The LORD has given a command concerning you, Nineveh: 'You will have no descendants to bear your name. I will destroy the carved images and cast idols that are in the temple of your gods. I will prepare your grave, for you are vile'" (Nahum 1:14).

MAMA MIA

My kids are spread out. There are 17 years between our oldest and youngest. I often quip that we had our first two kids as young fools and then God gave us a rather long break and we had our second set as, well, old fogies.

As I mommied my kids, I would find things about each child's stage of development that absolutely qualified it as the most difficult stage to date—until I reached the next stage. I'm sorry to burst anyone's bubble, but each stage brings its own set of unique challenges. Even the adult-child stage.

Fortunately for us, God also supplies His strength and wisdom through each stage. After all, it's not like God doesn't have any experience with prodigal children! But let me share what happened with one of my own prodigals.

I didn't want to believe my eyes. Just back from a weekend away, my husband and I were eager to relax and settle into a quiet evening at home. What we were confronted with was our older son, Chris, and his buddy frantically trying to conceal evidence of smoking pot, the same behavior that had gotten our younger son court-ordered out of our home.

God's Word tells us that we should always be "speaking the truth in love" (Ephesians 4:15), dealing with any problem or issue head on but without shame, blame or condemnation, but that day that attitude was absent.

"What are you doing?" my voice screeched, easily several decibels higher than an angry New York City taxi driver.

"Uh, hi, Mom . . . hi . . . uh, nothing . . ." came the jumbled, weak, unconvincing answer, one that until recently I had still been content to accept.

My head had been comfortably buried in the sand. Denial was a place of retreat.

By now my nose recognized the aroma of marijuana too well, even though Chris and his friend had done an admirable job of concealing the physical evidence. But they hadn't been able to open enough windows to fumigate the room before we came downstairs.

"What are you thinking?" I ranted, squinting at Chris.

"Uh, nothing," came the even weaker response—one final, feeble attempt to somehow desperately cling to the notion that they had not been caught lighting up in our home.

But this time we didn't buy it and what followed was an unemotional, matter-of-fact dictum. The line had been crossed one too many times, and Chris was promptly asked to move out.

It wasn't too long, however, before his anger turned to gratitude. He understood the universal lesson of reaping and sowing. He understood that loving sometimes came in the form of tough actions and choices. And he grew because of it.

As moms, we understand the connection between rebellion and destruction and how tough love can teach some valuable lessons, if we allow our kids to suffer the consequences of their poor and rebellious choices.

But like I imagine my Father in heaven despairs when I stray, I also despaired. I cried over Chris's poor choices, imploring God to both strengthen and comfort the two of us. And He did.

And He will do the same for you each step of the way as you parent children who—at some point—will stray. God will give you the strength that only He can provide.

Lightening the Mother Load: Straying off the straight and narrow is a natural part of life for moms and kids. I'm glad that God is always there to guide us back when we falter.

Musings for Moms:
- How many second chances do you give your kids before you finally draw the line?

- Have you ever loved tough? Was it harder for you or your child?

- Can you think of a time when you have experienced the equivalent of tough love from God?

Complain, Complain, Complain

Snapshot from Henrietta: The prophet Habakkuk wasn't afraid to question God directly. He went right to the top, without forming a committee for support. Habakkuk was distraught at the evil that was alive and well around him. In the not-too-distant past, King Josiah had been on the throne, and he was a good guy. He was responsible for spiritual renewal and reformation of God's Chosen People, but after he died, the spiritual renewal died as well. The one thing Habakkuk couldn't quite grasp was that God was going to deliver Judah into the hands of a nation even more raucous than itself. Did God really know what He was doing? But God was patient with Habakkuk (like He is with all His people) and finally got Habakkuk to see that He loved His people and ultimately had their best interest at heart. Habakkuk didn't need to fret; God had everything under control, which overjoyed him.

Mom Moments with Miss Mears

Her Synopsis:
Jesus Christ, the God of My Salvation

Her Suggested Bible Readings:
Habakkuk 1:1-17   Seeking and hearing from God
Habakkuk 2:12-14   A warning
Habakkuk 3:17-19   Hope endures

Momento: The whiny moanies need to be eliminated from our vocabularies.

Scripture: "How long, O LORD, must I call for help, but you do not listen? Or cry out to you, 'Violence!' but you do not save? Why do you make me look at injustice? Why do you tolerate wrong?

Destruction and violence are before me; there is strife, and conflict abounds" (Habakkuk 1:2-3).

MAMA MIA

Complaining, or the whiny moanies, as I refer to it, seem to be as prevalent among us moms as they are among our children. And it isn't any more attractive in us than it is in our kids.

Now, I have to admit to whining and moaning on my kids' behalf more than once (which, when misused, may be referred to as enabling or excusing behavior). However, God has taught me that He will defend our children if need be, if we leave it up to Him.

Not too long ago I was privy to a performance of parental whiny moanies worthy of an Oscar nomination. Unfortunately I understood it all too well, as it was an encore performance of one I had made years before.

"Where's the coach?" demanded Sue. She directed her question right at me, assuming I would know the answer. After all, it was my daughter who had convinced her daughter to join the swim team. "Where's the coach? Julie is not swimming breaststroke. She doesn't know how. Don't they know that? What are they thinking?" Sue paused briefly, coming up for air, and then launched into another tirade. "Julie came up to me in tears because they put her in breaststroke. My daughter does *not* swim breaststroke."

Sure enough, there was Julie sniffling, communicating her unhappiness over her scheduled events. She was accustomed to getting her way and knew her mom would take care of this for her.

I tried to explain the complexities of writing a meet lineup and how changing events two minutes before a meet wasn't the easiest thing to do, besides which the coaches were supervising warm-ups. But that didn't matter.

"Look at her. Look how upset she is," she said, her voice getting louder while drawing Julie closer to her side, letting her know that she would take care of it. "If they don't take her out of the event, I will take her off the team," she added for emphasis.

I made one more attempt at explaining the team concept of swimming and putting swimmers in events to fill out the roster, but I wasn't successful.

I found the coaches and warned them about the impending brouhaha, but the coaches weren't swayed, and they kept Julie in the breaststroke.

The coaches had won this round, but Sue and Julie hadn't learned from the experience. The next round of the fight dealt with a different matter but the same tactic. This time, it was Julie wailing the whiny moanies.

Julie was spending the weekend away with us, only she had packed as if she were sojourning for a month. I took one look at her suitcase and knew it wouldn't fit in the car.

"Julie," I said, "you're going to have to repack your suitcase. We don't have room for that suitcase in the car. I'll get you a smaller one to repack into."

The tears welled up in her eyes, and I had this overwhelming feeling of déjà vu. It was only a slight variation of the scene at the swimming pool: different opponent, but same tactic. And the same loss all over again.

The complaining hadn't changed the end result either time. And so it is with God. God is accustomed to humanity's complaints, but ultimately He can't and won't tolerate wrongdoing today any more than He could 2,000 years ago.

Lightening the Mother Load: Complaining is part of human nature. Divine nature is responding in grace and guiding the conversation to a positive win-win solution.

Musings for Moms:
• Read Habakkuk 1:3. Why do you think God tolerates wrong? Do you ever tolerate too much wrong from your children?

• How often do your children hear you complain? Do they believe complaining is an appropriate way to respond?

• Read Habukkuk 3:18-19. What does Habakkuk say to do when you feel like complaining?

ZEPHANIAH

You Are Not Alone

Snapshot from Henrietta: This book takes another look at God's kids going absolutely wild like an *Animal House* toga party. And He isn't happy. God speaks to His people through Zephaniah and tells them, "I will sweep away everything from the face of the earth" (Zephaniah 1:2). God has had it and won't take it anymore. No wiggle room for sin. But there is still hope as Zephaniah prophesies about a "remnant," a group who will seek God. The book ends with these hopeful words: "The LORD your God is with you, he is mighty to save. He will take great delight in you, he will quiet you with his love, he will rejoice over you with singing" (Zephaniah 3:17).

Mom Moments with Miss Mears

Her Synopsis:
Jesus Christ, a Jealous Lord

Her Suggested Bible Readings:
Zephaniah 1:1-3	Warnings
Zephaniah 1:14-18	The great day of the Lord
Zephaniah 3:9-17	God's redeeming love

Momento: Moms need the support of girlfriends and other moms who can be conduits of God's love.

Scripture: "The LORD your God is with you, he is mighty to save. He will take great delight in you, he will quiet you with his love, he will rejoice over you with singing" (Zephaniah 3:17).

MAMA MIA

Every mom needs a team of girlfriends. Sometimes we have girl-friends for a season; sometimes we have them for life. Regardless of the length of time we share, the women who walk alongside us through life are gifts from God.

There is something special and enduring about a friend who knows you, loves you, laughs with you, cries with you and is there for you in the same steadiness that God Himself is. And who still loves you despite your faults.

I recently got to celebrate friendship with such a special girl-friend. Not only did she go on vacation with me, my mom and younger daughter, but we loved each other even more at the end of the trip and could finish each other's sentences too! (We contem-plated whether perhaps there was a chance that we had been twins separated at birth.) I believe this happened because we were (and are) totally transparent with each other.

On our trip, we realized more and more that we have much in common—and not just our clothing size, although we can (and did) wear the same clothes and were willing to share everything down to a toothbrush (well, almost). We have survived the twos, the tens, the teens and even the twenties without too much gray hair (okay, we admit to some help in the color department). We truly had a delightful time!

Just like God takes great delight in us, we can both delight and take great delight in our true friends. There is no need to put on masks. We can be totally transparent, sharing tales too tall to be considered true, but too outrageous to make up. And isn't that how our relationship with God is too? Totally transparent? God laughs with us, cries with us and knows us down to the minutest detail of our being. He loves us and rejoices with us, walking alongside us through life.

I believe God sends us special friends to journey with through our lifetime. To me, they are like angels. And just as God has brought these angels into your life, He has most likely also used you as an angel in someone else's life.

Lightening the Mother Load: God sends us angels in the form of friends, who, like God, don't forsake us.

Musings for Moms:

· Is there someone in your life with whom you can be totally transparent? Do you see this person as an "angel"?

· Are you a friend who does not forsake? Why?

· What snapshot of God's love do we get in Zephaniah 3:17? Do you express that kind of love to your children?

Help Yourself!

Snapshot from Henrietta: Haggai is one of three minor prophets (Zechariah and Malachi are the other two) who prophesied after the Jews returned to Jerusalem from their exile in Babylon. Haggai was called by God to become the construction foreman for the reconstruction project of the Temple in Jerusalem.

Nehemiah had started the building project 15 years earlier, but the workers copped out and only managed to get the foundation completed. "They were few in number, poor, harassed by enemies and worse, they had lost the inner strength that comes from a joy in the Lord" (p. 341). They forgot about Jehovah and became more and more selfish, deciding instead to build their own houses and to let God's house rot.

Unfortunately, their spiritual condition rotted right along with it. God allowed some punishment along the way to get their attention focused on the job, and then He sent Haggai to get the job done. Haggai had better success than Nehemiah in coordinating the construction crew—but not until there had been a lot of heartache.

Mom Moments with Miss Mears

Her Synopsis:
Jesus Christ, the Desire of All Nations

Her Suggested Bible Readings:
Haggai 1:2-4	The time to build the Lord's house
Haggai 1:7-11	Building the Lord's house
Haggai 2:6-9	The promise of God's glory

Momento: How often do we develop a sense of entitlement and believe we deserve nice, new things when there are others that go without?

Scripture: "Then the word of the LORD came through the prophet Haggai: 'Is it a time for you yourselves to be living in your paneled houses, while this house remains a ruin?'" (Haggai 1:3-4).

MAMA MIA

I had become just a little bit too comfortable and complacent in my life (read "dissatisfied").

Surrounded by everyday comforts and conveniences of the Western world, I was in need of a reality check. I was taking far too much for granted. But I wasn't in the mood for that reality check until I seriously contemplated the addition of a sunroom to our house. Never mind that there were people living in huts with mud floors or people who didn't have any clean water to drink in the same hemisphere. They were a world away and not part of my reality.

I glanced out my deck door and decided it would be a great place to put a sunroom. There was a beautiful view out the back, and it would be the perfect spot to enclose a portion with a three-season sunroom.

Before long, I had it planned out down to the smallest details: the pictures on the wall, the type of tile on the floor and the over-stuffed rattan furniture. The table would have a glass top with wrought-iron scrolling supporting it, and perhaps there would be a hand-woven rug at each threshold. I could imagine sitting in my sunroom sipping coffee in the morning and winding down at the end of a busy day. It would be my God space. Then I had a radical paradigm shift.

I traveled to a developing country with a group of friends to serve as part of a medical brigade where we also did some home renovations. We were tucked away in the hills of a Central American country, where there was no regular electricity and only a limited amount of fresh water. The local laundromat was the stream that trickled through town.

I served as part of a team that put in cement floors. Not sunrooms, but cement floors. The typical home in these hills was not a 2,500-square-foot dwelling with every convenience and separate bedrooms for all the kids, but a 300-square-foot (maybe) shack with a dirt floor, an oven in a corner and no beds. Bathrooms and running water were also rarities.

Suddenly, I was embarrassed about my sunroom. It would have been bigger than the average home for a family of eight in that country. And as I mixed cement by hand for the next week, I became mortified that I had ever complained about the white tile floor in my kitchen. I had a kitchen, and it consisted of more than a fire pit in the corner that produced enough smoke to routinely set off smoke detectors (had there been any to set off).

I had a beautiful tile floor, not a dirt floor that turned into a mudslide for four months of every year during the rainy season. I had more than cornmeal that looked like animal feed for my sustenance. In fact, what went into my compost was probably better than what many people we served ate. A huge window as to how too many people in our world live had opened to me, and it readjusted my thinking.

It's easy to get sucked into the more, bigger, better, it's-all-about-me mentality, especially when the memory of another way of life fades. But all we need to do is return to God's Word to remind us that all we have really belongs to Him and that one day we will have to account for how we used His gifts.

Lightening the Mother Load: Allow courageous compassion to replace comfortable complacency, and add your hands to accomplishing God's work here on earth.

Musings for Moms:
• Do your children exhibit feelings of entitlement?

• Read Haggai 1:5-6. In what ways do these verses describe life in a nation of consumerism?

• What actions can you take as a parent to curb consumer habits that may feed into developing an attitude of entitlement in your children?

Mean Girls 101

Snapshot from Henrietta: Zechariah was Haggai's helper and cheerleader in getting the construction project of the Temple finished. By this time Haggai was getting pretty old and he needed the help of a young inspirational speaker. So Zechariah helped him out by painting a beautiful picture of what the people's relationship with God could be again. Dr. Mears points out that "Zechariah was the prophet of restoration and glory. . . . The glorious future rather than the sad present was his message" (p. 343). And it worked. The Temple was completed in just four years.

Mom Moments with Miss Mears

Her Synopsis:
Jesus Christ, the Righteous Branch

Her Suggested Bible Readings:
Zechariah 7:1-14   Justice and mercy
Zechariah 8:12-17   The Lord's love
Zechariah 10:1-12   The Lord's care

Momento: No mean girls allowed.

Scripture: "This is what the LORD almighty says: 'Administer true justice; show mercy and compassion to one another. Do not oppress the widow or the fatherless, the alien or the poor. In your hearts do not think evil of each other'" (Zechariah 7:9-10).

MAMA MIA

God's Word gives us a clear directive to not think evil of each other. This message is clear and consistent through God's entire history: We are to love one another and build each other up. Unfortunately, we aren't always as successful as we or God would like us to be, especially with the unlovely, or our enemies, translated "those who hurt us." Our natural inclination is to strike back, at least verbally. And words can sear the soul.

Women, moms included, can become catty and, without even realizing it, model this communication for our daughters, ensuring the continuation of the mean-girl mode of chitchat to the next generation. Our role as moms is not to allow the mean-girl mode to advance but to stop it in its tracks. Let me give you an example.

I could hear Tianna snickering from the other room where she and her friend were instant messaging a couple of friends. It didn't take me long to realize that in the instant messages, they were talking about each friend to the other behind her back.

Then the phone rang. "I'll get it. It's for me," Tianna yelled, making a beeline for the phone. The conversation that had been started on the computer screen was now being continued on the phone.

"Yeah, did you see that outfit she wore today? I can't believe she would wear that . . . and Jenny, she doesn't know how to dress either, and she thinks I look dorky sometimes," Tianna said.

I was then surprised to hear the very next words out of Tianna's mouth: "Oh, hi, Jenny. Sleep over at your house Friday? Sure, let me ask."

I got up, walked over and stood behind Tianna and her friend and glanced over their shoulders at the computer screen, which was minimized the minute I approached. I clicked the restore icon and brought the conversation back up on the screen.

"Mom," my daughter protested, "that's private and none of your business."

"Well," I answered, "actually it is my business."

She looked at me, clearly disagreeing.

"Honey," I started slowly, choosing my words with care, "mean words can hurt. You know that. It doesn't make me or God happy when any of us speak hurtful or mean words. I know sometimes I do, too, and if I do, I can ask Him to forgive me. But it's really important to always try to be kind, even if it's hard or someone has been mean to you first. I don't want you to be a mean girl. I want you to stop and think. If you guys are so quick to talk about Jenny and Kate behind their back, how do you know they aren't too? And then everyone's feelings are hurt."

I paused, allowing what I had said to sink in before I continued. "Mean girls can turn into mean women, and I don't want you to become someone who talks about other women behind their back. It can be really hurtful," I said, allowing my mind to remember times I had been involved in mean conversations from both sides.

Tianna and her friend both looked at me, their expression telling me they understood. I left the room quietly, and they went back to IMing their friends.

"Hey, Mom," Tianna called out from the other room, "we IM'd them both back and told them to forget what we had said. We were just in a funny mood." The phone rang again, and now the conversation continued on a different note.

For the moment, cattiness had been squelched, but just as the Israelites needed many reminders not to speak evil of others, I knew this too would be an ongoing message, not only for my girls, but for me as well.

Lightening the Mother Load: God loves us all equally; we need to love others compassionately and not allow ourselves to view others through the lens of comparison.

Musings for Moms:

· Is there ever a time it can be compassionate to talk about someone behind their back?

· When is the last time you talked about someone behind his or her back? Did you stop to think about it at all? If so, how did you feel? How do you feel when you find out someone has been talking about you behind your back?

· How can you model compassion to your children in everyday life? Start incorporating those ways into your life today.

What About Dad?

Snapshot from Henrietta: Malachi is the last of the 12 Minor Prophets and the last book of the Old Testament. We don't hear from God again for over 400 years. God was pretty tired of hearing the same old story over and over and over. The Jewish people had been home for a while (after their captivity in Babylon), but the Promised Land didn't look so great. Instead of finding land flowing with milk and honey, they found land that had been ransacked and pillaged. But far be it from them to accept any responsibility for the sad state of their beloved homeland. Jerusalem was in ruins and rather than examine their part in the mess, they started to grumble and groan as if they were back in the wilderness with Moses. They just couldn't see the parallels. No wonder God remained silent for a while. I think He was speechless that after all He had done, His beloved nation was still acting like a bunch of spoiled brats.

Mom Moments with Miss Mears

Her Synopsis:
Jesus Christ, the Sun of Righteousness

Her Suggested Bible Readings:
Malachi 1:1-5	Great is the Lord
Malachi 2:10-16	Guarding your spirit
Malachi 3:6	The Lord does not change
Malachi 4:2-3	God's healing for the righteous

Momento: For every child born to a mother there is also a father. Whether the dad is physically present in the home or not, kids need a relationship with their dad.

Scripture: "He will turn the hearts of the fathers to their children, and the hearts of the children to their fathers; or else I will come and strike the land with a curse" (Malachi 4:6).

MAMA MIA

In addition to our heavenly Father, we all have natural fathers too. Unfortunately, not all of us are able to have the kind of relationship with our natural dad that God desires. Some of us may have lost our dad at a young age (my mom's father was killed in an accident when she was six); some of us may have had an abusive father (I have a friend who suffered abuse at the hands of her father); and others may have had a dad who was absent due to a divorce or other obligations that took him away from the home for months or even years at a time (think of all the soldiers who are deployed on various tours of duty).

But even if our earthly dad is absent more often than he is present, God still yearns for kids to honor their father. Of course, like many other areas in life, it is easy to honor our dad if we have a good relationship with him. It is not quite so simple if that relationship has been tainted or interrupted. But God guides us through these waters as well. He promises to be "a father to the fatherless, a defender of widows. . . . God sets the lonely in families, he leads forth the prisoners with singing" (Psalm 68:5-6).

I have a friend who has been raising her six children as a single mom for the last several years. She was first widowed with two young children, and then she was once again left alone to raise her family when her second husband was sentenced to spend time in jail. Yet through these years of being both parents to her children, she has always honored Steve and taught her children to love and honor him as well. Even though the kids only knew their dad through sporadic weekend visits and phone conversations, they stayed as connected as they could with Steve. Linda is the one that made that happen.

I knew the kids loved their dad, and my heart broke for everything they were missing without him. Another leader in the family, another set of arms to give hugs, extra help with homework, someone to go out and play ball with, shared discipline and another set of ears—all ingredients of the special love of a dad.

Steve will be coming home in a couple of years, and God will reunite this family. Steve will once again be set into a family. For others the absence of their earthly father is permanent. But what is also permanent is the presence of their Father God.

Lightening the Mother Load: God wants to fill our love tanks and is happy to deliver a double portion if necessary.

Musings for Moms:

• In what ways can you influence your children to honor their father? Why is this still important if you are a single mom?

• How can your role as a mom encourage a stronger relationship between your kids and their dad?

• Think about the kind of relationship you had with your father. Are there ways your mom could have played a role in helping to improve it?

Special Delivery

Snapshot from Henrietta: Matthew is the first of the four Gospel writers. This book and the books of Mark and Luke are referred to as the Synoptic Gospels, meaning "taken together." Each Gospel (a word that means "good news") provides a different viewpoint of Jesus' life, offering the writer's unique perspective. Matthew wrote to the Jewish people "to show the Jews that Jesus is the long-expected Messiah, the Son of David, and that His life fulfilled the Old Testament prophecies" (p. 371).

The book of Matthew serves as the link between the Old and New Testaments. It begins with Christ's genealogy, which links Him with two of the Jewish people's all-time greats: David and Abraham. Matthew then goes on to talk about the life of Jesus in broad themes, solidly grounded in history. He also writes about the details of the life and ministry of Jesus from His revelation (who He was) to His resurrection, the entire time linking it to the Old Testament, which was important to his intended Jewish audience.

Mom Moments with Miss Mears

Her Synopsis:
Matthew Portrays Jesus Christ, the Promised Messiah

Her Suggested Bible Readings:

Matthew 1:18-25	The birth of Jesus
Matthew 5:13-16	The light of Christ
Matthew 6:19-21	Treasures in heaven
Matthew 13:16-23	Hearing and receiving God's message

Momento: Mary was not the first mother to conceive as an unwed mother, nor will she be the last.

Scripture: "This is how the birth of Jesus Christ came about: His mother Mary was pledged to be married to Joseph, but before they came together, she was found to be with child through the Holy Spirit. Because Joseph her husband was a righteous man and did not want to expose her to public disgrace, he had in mind to divorce her quietly" (Matthew 1:18-19).

MAMA MIA

God chose us as the mother of our children. Regardless of how our children joined our family, He chose us specifically to be a mom to the children He has given us. That places us in wonderful company. God also chose Mary (and Eve) and many, many other women who have walked before us in history to mother hand-chosen children.

God has gifted moms with the ability to love, to nurture and also to sacrifice. Sometimes the sacrifice is in putting the needs of others first as a mom. For Mary, the sacrifice was of her will and her reputation to honor God's choice to carry Jesus. She humbled herself and, as a result, she was blessed: "My soul glorifies the Lord and my spirit rejoices in God my Savior, for he has been mindful of the humble state of his servant. . . . For the Mighty One has done great things for me—holy is his name" (Luke 1:46-49).

For other moms, the sacrifice becomes the gift of selfless love that allows her to relinquish her child to the arms of another mother to raise and love. For example, somewhere halfway around the world in Vietnam, my daughter has another mother. I don't know much about her, but I imagine her story as best I can. I do know that she was young, about the same age as Mary was when she learned she was pregnant with Jesus. Also, like Mary, she was unwed and poor. And the similarities don't end there: Unwed pregnancies are viewed as a disgrace in my daughter's Vietnamese culture, much as they were in Galilee.

God chose a young, unwed Vietnamese mother to give birth to a daughter and then chose me to continue the job of nurturing and raising her that she could not continue. *Our* daughter.

I imagine Tianna's birth mother pregnant and struggling physically, emotionally and spiritually. I know she was weak and that

she came from a poor family who farmed rice and struggled to survive. Feeding one more mouth would have been difficult, even
aside from the shame that an unplanned pregnancy brought with
it. Life is hard in Vietnam.

I don't know what thoughts she carried along with her baby
about her future, but I choose to imagine a fierce love for her un-
born daughter, despite the circumstances of her conception. And
I imagine that it was this love that enabled Tianna's birth mother
to leave her newborn baby behind at the hospital. Hospital birth is
not the norm in Vietnam and was a huge step up from the typical
rural home birth. It was yet another indication of this mother's
protective love for her baby.

We waited and longed for the day to come that we would hold
and welcome our chosen daughter in our arms. We didn't know
God's plan, but He did, and He had everything worked out perfectly, just as He did with Mary and Jesus.

All of our children are chosen for us in God's perfect time, according to His perfect plan.

Lightening the Mother Load: There are no accidental pregnancies; they may be unplanned by us, but they are not unplanned
by God.

Musings for Moms:
· Have you or someone you know experienced an unplanned pregnancy? How was the news received?

· When our timing doesn't work out in the conceiving-a-child department, how likely are we to blame God? Do we stop to consider that God's timing involves a bigger picture than what we
can see?

· Do you think unwed mothers are stigmatized in our culture? Do
you think other cultures treat unwed mothers differently than
their wed counterpart? If so, how?

How May I Serve You?

Snapshot from Henrietta: Mark is the author of this Gospel, and unlike Matthew, he is most interested in what Jesus did. Because his intended audience was the Romans, the "equivalent of today's business people" (p. 390)—ordinary working-class people—it was important to connect Jesus with human lineage. The Romans were practical and valued common sense, so Mark's writing is direct and succinct. It is the shortest of the four Gospels and emphasizes the miracles that Jesus performed (20 are recorded in this Gospel). The book concentrates on the years of Jesus' ministry on earth. It gives us the model of servant leadership and how the needs of others can be met through simple service.

Mom Moments with Miss Mears

Her Synopsis:
Mark Portrays Jesus Christ, the Servant of God

Her Suggested Bible Readings:

Mark 1:1-8	Preparing the way of the Lord
Mark 9:23-37	Strengthening our belief
Mark 11:24	Belief and prayer

Momento: Moms spend a lot of their time serving others.

Scripture: "For even the Son of Man did not come to be served, but to serve, and to give his life as a ransom for many" (Mark 10:45).

MAMA MIA

As mothers, we don't need to look far to see that opportunities to serve abound. Moms are always being recruited as volunteers, more often than we care to admit. Playgroup team mom, dance-recital backstage mom, field-trip advisor, cleanup crew . . . you name it and chances are good that you've been there. The opportunities to help out seem endless.

Through these many opportunities to serve others, I am reminded of a universal truth: Everyone wants the high-profile job; no one really wants to clean the toilets. But what did Jesus have to say about service? "For even the Son of Man did not come to be served, but to serve" (Mark 10:45). Somehow after reading how Jesus washed His disciples' feet, I don't get the feeling that He only chose the glamour jobs.

I have a friend who is the exemplary model of Jesus-style service. In everything she does, her whole life exudes service. Her standard greeting is, "How are you? Is there anything I can do to make your day better?" And when she asks, she does so with genuine compassion, making eye contact and connecting with a gentle touch.

She serves in her chosen profession as well. She works as an elementary-school nurse, where she dispenses more than aspirin and Band-Aids. She dispenses love and compassion with words and gestures to children who may not receive as much kindness at home. I am sure Jesus is smiling down at her and at the end of her time she will hear, "Well done, good and faithful servant!" (Matthew 25:21).

But then I think of the all-too-common "servant" mom who prefers to be in the limelight as committee chair, publicly accepting praise for an entire team of workers without whom there wouldn't be any recognition at all.

Human nature too often pulls us toward the self-serving option rather than the serving-others option. But Jesus came to teach us otherwise. Our recognition and reward will come from Him, not from the head of the PTA or the soccer coach. "Whoever wants to become great among you must be your servant, and whoever wants to be first must be slave of all" (Mark 10:43-44).

Lightening the Mother Load: Life provides abundant opportunities to serve; it is one of God's divine purposes for us.

Musings for Moms:
• What is the most humble act of service you have ever performed?

• Think of a simple way you could serve and bless another mom, and then make a commitment to follow through in the next week.

• What barriers do you experience in serving others?

Hold On to Those Promises!

Snapshot from Henrietta: The third Gospel was written by Dr. Luke, who was not believed to be Jewish. If true, he would be the only non-Jew to author one of the books of the Bible. Luke was highly educated (as a physician), and he geared his narrative toward the Greeks, an audience who valued education, culture and philosophy.

Dr. Luke (himself Greek) was the perfect person to pen this Gospel linking Christ to the Greeks as the perfect Man. Luke consistently drew illustrations of compassion and healing into his Gospel account, consistent with his education as a doctor. But more than that he addresses the universal nature of Christ's interactions with others, especially those disdained by the Jews—women, children and Samaritans—underscoring the fact that He came to save *all* of mankind, not just the Jews.

The importance and expression of prayer is also emphasized. In fact, prayer is addressed more in the Gospel of Luke than in the other three Gospel accounts. In Luke 11, we read of how Jesus taught His disciples to pray. Dr. Mears notes that "Prayer is the expression of human dependence on God" (p. 401) and that "there is not enough private prayer" (p. 407). Prayer is the conduit of that expression of human dependence on God, for whom nothing is impossible.

Mom Moments with Miss Mears

Her Synopsis:
Luke Portrays Jesus Christ, the Son of Man

Her Suggested Bible Readings:

Luke 1:35-37	Nothing is impossible with God
Luke 1:46-56	Mary's song
Luke 3:16	Baptism of the Holy Spirit
Luke 6:27-49	Loving our enemies, judging others

Momento: It's not unusual for moms to get stuck in fear mode, factoring in only their own resources rather than divine intervention to solve problems.

Scripture: "For nothing is impossible with God" (Luke 1:37).

MAMA MIA

Have there been times you felt defeated and discouraged? (I know I have more than a few times!) When you feel that way, do you remember to cry out to God as a first step, remembering that nothing is impossible with Him?

How often do you remember to put prayer at the top of the list rather than as a last resort? I am reminded of a comment an acquaintance made a long time ago when she said with a sigh, "Well, I've tried everything else, I don't know what to do . . . I guess I should pray."

I will admit that I don't always go to the Lord first. Sometimes I try to figure out solutions to problems myself, becoming an expert at trying to force square pegs through round holes. It is only when I get to the place where I give up and say, "Okay, Lord, I am handing this over to You, I am done," that my "solutions" appear pretty limited, puny and shortsighted compared to what God can do.

I was recently faced with a daunting challenge. We'll just say I felt like David facing a huge Goliath, and I allowed fear and negativity (evil distractions) to get the upper hand. Have you ever been there? It was at that point, when things looked pretty bleak, that I groaned out to God, "Help me, please. I know You can't stand lies, and You are truth, love and justice personified, but I am just feeling so defeated. Please, Lord, help me . . ."

And a couple of wonderful things happened, one via email and another via a phone call to remind me of the powerful truth that nothing is impossible with God. A friend sent me an email that reminded me of David and Goliath, specifically the question, "Who is this uncircumcised Philistine that he should defy the armies of the living God?" (1 Samuel 17:26). And I encourage you to ask basically the same question: "Who indeed?" As followers of the living God, when we yield to His leadership, the weak become strong and the young shepherds defeat the mighty giants. What seems impossible in our view is possible with God.

Then I got a phone call from a friend, asking how things were going in my personal battlefield and asking me for prayer for the Goliath she was facing. Mine happened to involve litigation, hers a health crisis. And I was able to point her to the encouragement I had already received.

"Mary," I said, this time confident in my ability to trust that my situation was not impossible with God, so neither was hers, "just think of the many ways God has already been faithful to you and the situations He has seen you through. I'm sure there has been a situation in the past that you felt was impossible, and God provided a solution."

I was thinking of examples from my own life when she answered, "Yes, that's true." She paused and then asked, "Do you have a Bible there? I am at the post office and don't have access to one, but I was just reminded of something. Turn to Psalm 77."

I went downstairs, propped the cordless phone under my chin and flipped to the seventy-seventh psalm.

"Now start reading," she said.

And what unfolded was a beautiful poem of crying out to God for help, remembering His answers from the past, and the acknowledgment of His holy and miraculous ways.

"Now look at the middle part," she said. "See those questions? There are six of them."

"Will the Lord reject forever? Will he never show his favor again: Has his unfailing love vanished forever? Has his promise failed for all time? Has God forgotten the merciful? Has he in anger withheld his compassion?" (Psalm 77:7-9). As I read and reflected on these questions, I answered each one "no."

"That's right," Mary answered. "I remember when I was going through an impossible time and I went to this psalm and actually wrote the word 'no' behind each of these questions and claimed the promises."

And I knew I needed to do the same. It was yet one more perfectly timed reminder that nothing is impossible with God as we continue to wrestle and groan—at times even doubting—yet at the same time claim His holy ways and ability to perform miracles.

Absolutely nothing is impossible for God. Don't be afraid to face your Goliath; God will sustain you. Groan out to Him.

Lightening the Mother Load: We are often more interested in our plans than God's plans for answering our prayers, but we need to allow Him to fulfill us as we wait for His answers. With God, nothing is impossible.

Musings for Moms:

· Has there been a time in your life when you were confronted with what seemed like an impossible situation? Did you pray for a solution, or just forge ahead and try to figure one out yourself?

· When confronted with difficulties, do you generally try to figure out a solution for yourself first, or do you hand it over to God and wait for His response?

· Do you have a hard time believing that *all* things are possible with God? What has helped you to have more trust in this promise about God?

The Ultimate Teacher

Snapshot from Henrietta: John, the author of the fourth Gospel, has a singular purpose: "John wrote to prove that Jesus was the Christ, the promised Messiah (for the Jews) and the Son of God (for the Gentiles), and to lead believers into a life of divine friendship with Him" (p. 419). He wanted people to believe beyond a shadow of a doubt that Jesus was the Messiah and the Son of God. The word "believe" is used 98 times in the book of John. There is no question that John was an evangelist!

Highlights of the Gospel of John include the story of Jesus' first miracle, when He turned water into wine and saved the day for a huge wedding party (John 2:1-10); a story about Jesus being really angry, a somewhat different perspective than many of us are accustomed to (John 2:12-16); and several stories of miraculous healings. The Gospel ends with the story of Christ's resurrection, the greatest miracle of all.

Mom Moments with Miss Mears

Her Synopsis:
John Portrays Jesus Christ, the Son of God

Her Suggested Bible Readings:

John 3:5-6	Entering God's kingdom
John 3:16	God's gift
John 6:29,43-44,63	Spiritual life
John 14:1-4,25-26	The coming of the Comforter

Momento: Children aren't the only ones who need teachers; moms need teachers too.

Scripture: "But the Counselor, the Holy Spirit, whom the Father will send in my name, will teach you all things and will remind you of everything I have said to you" (John 14:26).

MAMA MIA

God sent us the power of His Holy Spirit, so we would not need to go through life alone.

My life changed forever in June 2001, when God captured my heart and I received the gift of His Spirit to guide me. When I finally met God, I was in desperate need of a mentor and Savior. My theology and life of self-sufficiency were crumbling, but God was there to pick up the pieces and reshape them according to His plan. Up until that time, I had thought I could fix my own life with a steady diet of self-help books.

I was still searching for the perfect title when, one day in June, my son Chris had a suggestion for me. "Hey, Mom, check it out," he said from the other room, his voice interrupting my thoughts. "This guy on TV is talking about a really cool book. I think you should read it."

"I don't need more books," I shot back. I had a collection of titles from Steven Covey to Dr. Phil, but so far none had helped.

"No, Mom, really!" his voice insisted from the other room. "This book sounds really cool. You oughta get it. It might help." He knew I was going through a difficult season and happened to be flipping through the TV channels and caught the tail end of an interview with Bruce Wilkinson, author of *The Prayer of Jabez,* on *The Today Show.*

Chris persisted, affected by what he had heard. "Hey, check it out. This book has changed tons of lives. Maybe it could change yours too."

I was unconvinced and ignored his suggestion, until the little book he had mentioned resurfaced a couple of days later when I was back at the bookstore searching for more titles. I had forgotten about the one Chris had mentioned a couple of days earlier, but God was just about to remind me.

While I was standing in line—waiting to check out—a woman came bursting through the door, her eyes darting around, searching for the title in question.

"Do you have that book . . . you know," she said urgently, "that book . . . that book . . . that little book everyone is talking about . . . *The Prayer of Jabez?*"

A chord of recognition registered inside my head. That was the book Chris had been talking about.

As I approached the checkout counter, the clerk gestured to a little stand propped up directly in front of me. There it was. *The Prayer of Jabez,* perfectly positioned for purchase. The clerk handed the frantic woman a copy and then turned to wait on me.

I picked up a copy. "Have you read this?" I asked the clerk, the skepticism clear in my voice.

"No, not yet, but we can't keep it in stock."

I fingered a copy, glanced at the price and decided my life was worth the ten-dollar sticker price.

With the purchase of that little book, I embarked on the path of my spiritual journey. I knew that I had been searching, but I wasn't sure what for. There was something missing, and all my attempts at self-correction and control had fallen short. Harmony was absent. The infrastructure of my family was crumbling.

Curiosity and hope fueled my desire to read the book. I couldn't imagine that such a small volume could have such a huge impact on people's lives. But I read and reread, and I began each day praying the prayer of Jabez.

At first the words were stiff and mechanical, punctuated with unbelief. With time, the words became more sincere. "Bless me indeed. Please bring some healing to my hurting soul. Protect me from evil so that I may not cause pain." My words took on yet greater urgency and sincerity. My perception of events changed. I felt open to God in a way I had never experienced before, and remarkable changes started to happen.

Just a couple of weeks later, a good friend invited me to church and handed me a little card with a prayer written on it. "Here," she said. "Our pastor just finished a series of messages on this prayer."

I glanced at the card and there were the words to *The Prayer of Jabez.* I let out a startled yelp and told her I would love to come to church. She had gently and persistently invited me to worship with her family for years, but I had not been ready.

My friend worshiped at a Mennonite church, and I really wasn't sure what to expect. I do know, though, that I never anticipated the experience that I was about to have.

As I listened to the praise and worship, I was profoundly affected. When the pastor gave his message, I felt as though he was speaking directly to me. And an overwhelming sense of love and serenity settled over me.

The pastor ended the message with an invitation to accept Christ and His healing power and love. I was desperate to respond yet I felt unable to move. God, however, had everything under control.

The next part of the service was a time of sharing and without even realizing it, I stood and took the microphone into my hand. Through choked-back tears I expressed my pain, confusion and desire for Christ's healing love in my life. I sensed overwhelming relief but also uncertainty. I felt comforted in a way I had never been before—as if I had "come home."

But now what? What had just happened? I didn't understand the gift I had just received, that the power of Jesus' love and Sprit had just entered me.

With each day since that Sunday, God has revealed more of what it means to have Christ in my life. His mercy, His love and His grace have become woven into the tapestry of my life through the gift of His Holy Spirit, the Counselor who is with me all the time.

And the Counselor is also there to help you in your parenting journey. Take advantage of the things He has to teach you.

Lightening the Mother Load: God yearns to enlarge your territory, not through self-help, but through His help.

Musings for Moms:
- What resources do you turn to in your parenting journey? How often is God on the list?

- Do you own any Bible study books? Any devotionals (other than the one in your hands)? How can these books help you learn more about God?

· Do you recall a time when you first encountered the Holy Spirit? Did you realize it was the Holy Spirit at the time? Have you accepted Jesus as your teacher, companion and savior in life? If so, how did you feel about that experience? If you haven't, would you be willing to express that desire to Him now?

A Family Affair

Snapshot from Henrietta: Acts is really a continuation of Luke's Gospel. Luke is also the author of the book of Acts. In his Gospel account, Luke writes about what Christ began to do on earth; in Acts, he shows what Christ continued to do by the power of the Holy Spirit. The book of Acts opens right where the Gospel of John leaves off: with Christ's ascension. The Gospels tell about Christ's teachings; "in Acts we see the effect of His teachings on the acts of the apostles. . . . It records the acts of the Holy Spirit through the apostles" (p. 440).

The Holy Spirit appears in every chapter of Acts, popping up more than 70 times. The gospel spread with unbelievable speed throughout the ancient world, despite unimaginable persecution. The mind-boggling account of the conversion of Saul, a Pharisee to the Pharisees who was bent on killing as many of the new believers as he could, is told in chapter 9 of this book. Through his conversion he became Paul, the humble apostle who recorded more than two-thirds of the New Testament. The book of Acts is a travelogue of Paul's missionary travels.

Mom Moments with Miss Mears

Her Synopsis:
Acts Portrays Christ, the Living Lord

Her Suggested Bible Readings:

Acts 2:44-47	The model of church
Acts 4:29-30; 14:3	Boldness in belief
Acts 5:29,38-39	Success in pleasing God
Acts 16:30-31	A promise for belief

Momento: Some families come to faith in Christ through one family member. This is a powerful promise for those moms who walk solo in the journey of faith.

Scripture: "He then brought them out and asked, 'Sirs, what must I do to be saved?' They replied, 'Believe in the Lord Jesus, and you will be saved—you and your household' " (Acts 16:30-31).

MAMA MIA

Not every mom is married to a spiritual leader. Sometimes the husband is absent physically; other times he is absent spiritually. In either of these families, the mother becomes the one to lead her family to God.

Although spiritual leadership can be lonely, know that you are not alone and that God will honor your desire to lead and love by example. He will walk alongside you. I know this for a fact. My husband does not yet share my faith, and there is nothing I can do to accept Christ's gift for him. I can only pray for him and live my faith out in a way that makes it irresistible.

What does it look like to assume the spiritual helm for your family? It looks like love. "The measure in which Christians love one another is the measure in which the world believes in them or their Christ" (p. 432). Loving others will woo them to Christ, as long as it is His unconditional love we are conduits of—loving in humility, loving gently, loving in service, loving the unlovely, loving when it is inconvenient, loving when we don't get our way, loving sacrificially, loving extravagantly.

I knew my faith had made an impression on my husband the day he said to me, "Kathy, I really like the person you are becoming," and then turned bright red in startled embarrassment at his backhanded compliment. But to tell you the truth, his words were beautiful to me, because they meant that he could see a change in me.

And that is what happens when Christ lives within us: A transformational change takes place. And if we want to see this transformation take place in others, we need to persevere not only in loving them but also in praying to God for them. We need His help to soften the heart in those we hope to love into the Kingdom.

Prayer is up to us; the rest is up to God.

Lightening the Mother Load: Continue to love others, including nonbelieving spouses, with God's love. God desires to adopt into His family all those who don't yet recognize Him as "their" Father.

Musings for Moms:
- Did you grow up with faith having been passed down from generation to generation, or is exploring a life with Christ new for you?

- Is there one family member in particular who was influential in your faith walk?

- Do you view yourself as a spiritual leader? Why or why not?

New Strength

Snapshot from Henrietta: Romans is the first of the epistles (or letters) in the New Testament. There are 21 letters, and Paul wrote 13 of them. This one was written to the Romans, hence the name. Paul was perfectly qualified as a missionary. He was a Roman citizen, had a Greek education and grew up Hebrew, yet after his miraculous conversion, he trusted solely in the grace he received directly from Christ (that head-on collision he had on the road to Damascus). Paul really needed to be several places at the same time preaching the gospel, but since that wasn't possible, there were times a letter had to suffice.

The book of Romans clarifies the gospel to the new believers in Rome, many of whom had chosen some rather self-serving interpretations of how to live out their faith (not that anything like that happens today!). Dr. Mears notes, "The book of Romans tells us of God's method of making guilty people good. The key of this great thesis is found in Romans 1:16-17: The Person of the gospel—Christ; the Power of the gospel—'power of God'; the Purpose of the gospel—'for salvation'; the People to whom sent—'to everyone'; the Plan of acceptance—'to everyone who believes'; the Particular result—'the righteous will live by faith'" (p. 462).

Mom Moments with Miss Mears

Her Synopsis:
Romans Portrays Christ, Our Righteousness

Her Suggested Bible Readings:

Romans 1:11-12; 2:7	Encouragement through faith
Romans 5:1-5	Justified by faith
Romans 8:26-28	Faith and prayer in all things
Romans 12	Living sacrifices

Momento: Our strength comes from God, not from yelling louder.

Scripture: "Do not conform any longer to the pattern of this world, but be transformed by the renewing of your mind. Then you will be able to test and approve what God's will is—his good, pleasing and perfect will" (Romans 12:2).

MAMA MIA

When we join God's parenting team, He will equip us with new skills. Our old and ineffective patterns (like screaming, yelling and threatening, in my case) will be transformed into new ways that are pleasing to God (like realizing that it is sufficient to state the truth and then stand by it firmly). The change doesn't come naturally and may, in fact, yield some strange looks from those who don't yet understand this principle.

Consider discipline. Discipline is nothing new to God; He has been disciplining His children for years. And, just like the Israelites, I am also—at times—a slow learner.

Have you ever repeated the same threat or ineffective disciplinary technique over and over, hoping for a different outcome? I know I have. I hate to admit it, but I used to be a real yeller and the queen of empty threats. Somehow I thought if I repeated myself in a voice at least 10 decibels louder or an octave higher, it would yield my desired results. I was wrong.

But I empathize with those moms who may lose it in the middle of the grocery store (or other public place) and add a swat to a bottom when they think no one is looking. I've been there too—most recently at a European monastery. But God gave me His supernatural strength to try a different approach.

On a recent trip, I agreed to share my new camera with my daughter. The terms of the agreement between us were straightforward enough. She could use it all she wanted, but I got first dibs while we were on the trip. When we returned home, it would be hers as part of her birthday gift.

No problem . . . that is, until I wanted to take photos at a beautiful sixteenth-century church—not exactly the place one wants to have a disciplinary standoff with a strong-willed child. She became loud (and attracted the wordless yet pointed attention of one of the monks); I held my ground and repossessed the camera. She yelled louder. I continued to hold my ground but admit to wishing I could disappear. And this went on well into the afternoon and evening. But God gave me His strength and I didn't give in.

There were lessons in this for both of us. For my daughter, it was to learn that she is not in control and cannot get her way by screaming. And for me, it was that when I transform my mind to His way and lean on Him, He will give me strength.

Lightening the Mother Load: God will give you the strength to help you lighten the mother(ing) load in all areas!

Musings for Moms:
- Have there been times when you have yielded to the pressure of giving in to your child in a situation when you haven't wanted to? Do you have trouble standing firm?

- If you continue to allow your child to get his or her way, how much more difficult do you think it will be when you finally transform your approach?

- What type of disciplinarian are you? How have you consulted God and His Word in forming your approach to discipline?

The Gong Show

Snapshot from Henrietta: Paul had spent a year and a half in Corinth, a booming Greek city, supporting his missionary work by working at his trade as a tentmaker. As a matter of fact, he had hooked up with a couple of other Jewish tentmakers, Aquila and Priscilla, and worked and hung out with them the entire time he was preaching the gospel to both Jews and Gentiles. Unfortunately, Corinth was party central, and after Paul moved on, the church at Corinth began to be influenced by the worldliness of the city. As Dr. Mears writes, "It was all right for the church to be in Corinth, but it was fatal when Corinth got into the church" (p. 474). Lust, greed, and gossip were just a few of the aspects of the Corinthians' out-of-control lascivious living that needed to be corrected. So Paul pulled out his pen, and they were the next group to get a letter.

Mom Moments with Miss Mears

Her Synopsis:
First Corinthians Portrays Jesus Christ, Our Lord

Her Suggested Bible Readings:
1 Corinthians 2:10-16   The Spirit of God
1 Corinthians 3:11,16   The foundation is Christ and we are
                         His temple
1 Corinthians 13:1-13   The story of love
1 Corinthians 15:58   Work in God is not in vain

Momento: How often do moms speak the language of "nag"?

Scripture: "If I speak in the tongues of men and of angels, but have not love, I am only a resounding gong or a clanging cymbal" (1 Corinthians 13:1).

MAMA MIA

I love my children, but sometimes when I talk to them, I don't always sound like I like them. Sometimes I end up speaking the language of "nag." But God doesn't nag us, so why do I nag my kids? Do I really enjoy sounding like "a resounding gong or a clanging cymbal"? Do I want my voice to reverberate, ricocheting loud and discordant reminders inside my children's ears? Do I want my kids to pick up this unpleasant habit?

God instructs me to make sure I communicate in love. Of course, if I did that all the time, nagging would be eliminated. Nagging is such an easy language to learn, and it always starts innocently.

To teach my little ones to pick up after themselves, I could have happily sung, "Clean up, clean up, everybody do your *share* . . ." Instead, I started with a series of questions: "Did you . . . ?"; "Would you . . . ?"; "Could you . . . ?" I repeated these over and over, sort of like a resounding gong or a clanging cymbal.

After cleaning up, the questions turn to homework, feeding the pets, studying for final exams, getting to work on time, and finally getting a "real" job.

The most recent topic of conversation in which I ended up sounding more like a clanging cymbal than an encouraging mom had to do with the current job status of my younger son. He was going to be finished with college soon but didn't have a job lined up yet. Nagging was my way of taking matters into my own hands rather than allowing God to work His plan in my son's life.

I was with Matt at an orthopedic appointment, waiting for the doctor to come into the exam room, when I launched into my concerns about his future.

"Matt, I think it's time you get a real job when you graduate. You know, one that pays more than nine dollars an hour and has benefits." (This was not Matt's first orthopedic experience, so benefits would be an important part of his future.) "So, yeah, a real job, one that will use your degree and won't be seasonal—one with benefits."

I added for emphasis, "You know, one that goes year round." I cringed as soon as the words left my mouth, but it was too late. They had already escaped and I couldn't recapture them.

Matt smiled, looking down at his left wrist—trying to improve its range of motion. "Yeah, like wilderness programs," he finished my unspoken thought and continued. "I know, Mom, you've said so a million times." He was right; I had. Nagging wasn't doing anything to strengthen the mother-son bond.

"Hi, Matt. I'm Dr. Klena." The doctor entered the room and introduced himself. Saved. The conversation was over for the moment. But I knew I wouldn't let it rest.

I did resurrect the conversation, but when I did, I was able to do so with more grace, allowing Matt to express his dreams and desires instead of my own. Slowly I communicated with the soft sounds of love instead of the harsh tones of blame. I should have realized that God had a plan for Matt all along—it just didn't match with mine. I still have a hard time not pounding square pegs through round holes. Can you relate?

Matt has been able to spend some time with my aging mom, who is transitioning to another phase of life. If he had taken a full-time job immediately after graduation, he wouldn't have been available to provide her with his support and companionship while also working part-time.

I couldn't have planned or foreseen this in a million years, but God did, and once again, He reminded me that His ways, although we don't always understand them, are better. What we need to do is love.

Lightening the Mother Load: God's vision and plan always encompass more than we can imagine. Step back and allow God to place you and use you in His story as it unfolds.

Musings for Moms:
- Has nagging ever been effective for you in getting what you want? At what cost?

- Do your children listen to you when you speak to them in a soft tone of voice?

- How adept at putting square pegs into round holes are you? What would help you do things in a better way?

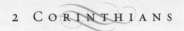

Comfort to Comfort

Snapshot from Henrietta: One letter wasn't enough to help correct the problems at the church in Corinth. Paul had to write a follow-up letter to make sure he got his point across. This second letter is part encouragement and part rebuke. While most of the Corinthians had responded well to his first letter (and he wanted to encourage them), many others had started spreading rumors about him, casting doubt on his reputation and his authority as an apostle. (That is where the rebuke came in.) The book also has a biographical quality, filling us in on more of Paul's life, again showing that God can use and equip anyone to serve Him.

Mom Moments with Miss Mears

Her Synopsis:
Second Corinthians Portrays Jesus Christ, Our Sufficiency

Her Suggested Bible Readings:

2 Corinthians 1:3-7; 7:6-7	Comforting others
2 Corinthians 2:15	The aroma of Christ
2 Corinthians 4:17-18	Fixing our eyes on faith
2 Corinthians 6:4-6	Bearing hardships
2 Corinthians 10:17-18; 12:9-10	Boasting in the Lord

Momento: Don't offer comfort or empathy, unless you really have walked in the other person's shoes.

Scripture: "Praise be to the God and Father of our Lord Jesus Christ, the Father of compassion and the God of all comfort, who comforts us in all our troubles, so that we can comfort those in any trouble with the comfort we ourselves have received from God" (2 Corinthians 1:3-4).

MAMA MIA

I haven't always been grateful for the challenging and difficult experiences in my life. Yet I know that God will never waste a hurt. He will use every one of my miseries as an opportunity to minister if I am willing to share.

What unique experiences has God brought you through that you in turn can use to help encourage someone else? The empathy, encouragement and advice from someone who has walked the same path have the credibility that only experience brings. So I looked to other moms who had "been there, done that" through each of the stages as I approached a new frontier with my growing kids.

When it came to descriptions of labor contractions, I was inclined to believe my girlfriends who were moms more so than my childless childbirth educator.

When negotiating the terrible twos, my friend who had two-year-old twins was my go-to gal. "They say 'no' all the time, live in a perpetual tug-of-war and are constantly undressing and climbing out of their crib and onto the windowsills." I made a mental note to put child locks on my windows and move my own two-year-old to a ground-floor bedroom.

The experience of other preschool moms taught me the value of play as education and allowed me to relax and enjoy the magical years of young childhood with my daughters without fretting about whether my choice of preschool would influence their future college admissions.

As the first day of kindergarten approached, I trusted the judgment of moms who had already had the bittersweet experience of seeing their child off to the first day of school. I understood the message that a chapter in my child's life had just begun, while for me, another chapter had just finished and the empty nest would come soon enough. Only a mom who has endured the same hurts and broken dreams that I have is qualified to hug me and comfort me, because she can convey her understanding—an understanding that I can believe.

God can also use us and our experiences to touch someone else. We can also be that mom, that beacon of hope to another mom who travels the parenting path two paces behind us. We can use our own set of experiences to reach out with a helping hand of comfort in the same way that God extends His hand to us.

Lightening the Mother Load: God won't waste any experiences; He will use all of them to help encourage others. Allow yourself to be His messenger of comfort.

Musings for Moms:
· Have you ever offered advice to another mom when you didn't really know what you were talking about?

· What tough experiences as a mom has God given you that uniquely qualify you to comfort others who are traveling the same difficult journey?

· How can you use your weaknesses to encourage other moms?

People Pleasers

Snapshot from Henrietta: The keyword for Galatians, yet another letter penned by Paul, is "grace." Grace, grace and more grace. Not rules, but grace. Of course there were those who didn't agree with this and tried to superimpose Jewish law on the message of grace. These were Jewish Christians who wanted to add all the Jewish rules to the message of grace; and the people at Galatia were pretty gullible (and fickle too), so they believed these false teachers and gave Paul a hard time. So it was time to write another letter, this time explaining to the new believers that the only thing necessary for salvation was to believe in the Lord Jesus Christ. Period. Legalism, he explained, was not a necessary part of believing in Jesus.

Mom Moments with Miss Mears

Her Synopsis:
Galatians Portrays Jesus Christ, Our Liberty

Her Suggested Bible Readings:
Galatians 2:6-10	God doesn't judge by external appearances
Galatians 3:2-3,14,25	Faith through the Spirit
Galatians 5:4-6,13,26	Faith through love, not law
Galatians 6:1-7	Doing good to all

Momento: The truth of the matter is that we are people pleasers who are trying to win approval from others—even from those closest to us.

Scripture: "Am I now trying to win the approval of men, or of God? Or am I trying to please men?" (Galatians 1:10).

MAMA MIA

"Religion is the best people can do. Christianity is the best God can do" (p. 499). Religion concerns itself with rules and regulations, ensuring that we will never be good enough, no matter how much we do or how much we try. The goal of perfection is eternally elusive when chased after in our own power. The only way to perfection is through the work of Christ on the cross.

"Know that man is not justified by observing the law, but by faith in Jesus Christ. . . . By observing the law no one will be justified" (Galatians 2:16). Justification comes through faith.

Similar to the tension that exists in putting our faith in works rather than grace is the human tendency to seek approval from other people instead of from God. But when we do that, we carry a false message of religion into our relationships.

This can show up in subtle ways, such as fishing for a compliment. "What do you think of my new haircut?" I ask my friends if they don't notice it quickly enough. Other times it is not so subtle, like when we desperately look for affirmation from someone close to us (such as a husband, best friend or parent) and their response, or lack thereof (or, worse yet, criticism), crushes us when it is not what we had hoped for.

"You didn't really let your kid watch that movie did you? Did you lose your mind?" your girlfriend and mother of your daughter's best friend asks.

"You can't wear that; it shows those extra pounds you just put on," your husband comments, thinking he will save you from embarrassment, but instead sending you into the dredges of despair.

"Why would you want to retire in Roatan? It's so far away from everything and *backward*" was my mom's remark when I was excited to share the dream of future retirement on a Caribbean island with her.

The issue here isn't as much about other people's responses as much as it is about us turning to God and His ever-present, unwavering and eternal love and delight in us. So instead of seeking approval from others, seek approval from God. Turn to God with your hopes, dreams and desires, and delight yourself in His opinion.

God is enthralled by you and your beauty (see Psalm 45:11). Turn to Him only to affirm your worth.

Lightening the Mother Load: God's opinion is the one that matters; live to please Him, not people.

Musings for Moms:
- Read Galatians 5:22-23, which lists the fruits of the Spirit. How are peace and self-control related to seeking approval?

- How does trying to please others interfere with living out faith in God?

- Read Galatians 3:26. How do we become children of God? How can you teach your children to seek God's approval?

Referee to the Rescue

Snapshot from Henrietta: Ephesus was the site of another one of Paul's early church plants. They needed instruction too, so it was again time to pull out the papyrus and writing instrument. Even though they had started out with fervor and commitment to their beliefs, they needed some guidance to prevent them from slipping back into pagan worship. Particularly problematic was worship to the Greek god Artemis (you can read about this in Acts 19), so Paul wrote this letter. It is all about how to live in harmony with Christ under His grace, and it is about living in unity with other believers in the Body who are culturally or ethnically different.

Mom Moments with Miss Mears

Her Synopsis:
Ephesians Portrays Jesus Christ, Our All in All

Her Suggested Bible Readings:
Ephesians 1:1-11   Adopted by Christ
Ephesians 2:8   Saved by grace
Ephesians 4:1-32   Unity in the Body of Christ

Momento: In addition to all the other roles a mom has, she is also chief referee.

Scripture: "Make every effort to keep the unity of the Spirit through the bond of peace" (Ephesians 4:3).

MAMA MIA

One of the great challenges moms have is to model unity and the bond of peace. As moms, we get daily practice in peace building as we referee our kids' squabbles. I know I have been called on to fill the role of chief referee more than once, and even moms who only have one child aren't exempt from this role. Arguments and disagreements erupt all around us as part of daily life. Can you relate?

"Mo-o-o-o-o-m," I heard the wail coming from one of the upstairs bedrooms. I couldn't immediately tell which daughter was summoning my services, but I knew it would only be seconds before I would hear another call for help.

"Mom. Mom, Mom! . . . tell her to get out of my room!" came the desperate plea of my older daughter.

The disagreement was nothing new. Peace and unity just didn't seem to be part of their vocabulary in approaching each other. So for what seemed like the fifth time that morning, I trudged up the stairs to serve as referee.

Weary from the ongoing squabbles, my voice clearly revealed my energy level. "What seems to be the problem this time?" I sighed as I reached the top of the staircase.

"She came in my room without asking," Tianna scowled at Nicole.

"She took my favorite CD without asking," Nicole retorted.

"Well, you can't listen to it anyway; you broke your CD player," Tianna shot back.

It was my turn to step in—trying to restore peace and harmony.

"It sounds like neither one of you is treating the other with respect and asking for permission," I paused, waiting to see if my words registered. "Both of you need to ask permission; whether it is borrowing a CD, or going into each other's room—you need to ask if it's okay first."

"Okay, Mom," they said in unison. Tianna reluctantly returned the CD, and Nicole backed out of Tianna's room. Peace had been restored—for the moment anyway.

As I returned downstairs, I thought about unity and the value of peace and reconciliation to God. God yearns for us to have unity with Him and with each other. One of the ways we as moms can serve Him is to serve as peacemakers within our own families.

Lightening the Mother Load: Peace can be achieved one person at a time. God is in the reconciliation business; allow it to begin with you.

Musings for Moms:
- How often do you serve as a referee with your children? Do you view yourself as a peacemaker?

- What steps can you take to build more unity within your family?

- List three ways you can model for your children peacekeeping with others.

Thanks, No Matter What

Snapshot from Henrietta: Philippians is yet another letter from Paul, but this time it is a love letter, not one full of rebuke, exasperation or even instruction. These guys in Philippi seemed to get it right, and Paul is happy to write them in affirmation of that. Paul is full of joy, despite writing this letter from prison, chained to his guard. He reminds his readers of joy and uses "joy" or "rejoice" 16 times in this letter. He wrote from the heart; he experienced the joy he was writing about! The epistle both begins and ends with gratitude, another great reminder to us today about how to start and finish our day.

Mom Moments with Miss Mears

Her Synopsis:
Philippians Portrays Jesus Christ, Our Joy

Her Suggested Bible Readings:

Philippians 1:9-11	Thanksgiving and prayer
Philippians 2:1-5	Joy in Christ
Philippians 4:4-7,11-13	Joy and contentment

Momento: Gratitude helps shape and soften our hearts.

Scripture: "I know what it is to be in need, and I know what it is to have plenty. I have learned the secret of being content in any and every situation, whether well fed or hungry, whether living in plenty or in want" (Philippians: 4:12).

MAMA MIA

How many of us can truly identify with these words of the apostle Paul: "I know what it is to be in need, and I know what it is to have plenty" (Philippians 4:12). I know there have been times when I feel like I am in need, but there are many more times I can acknowledge having plenty. I usually don't have to look too far to find someone who is not as well off as me. But sometimes God gives us a striking example so that the lesson is deeply impressed on our heart.

I was part of a mission team serving on mainland Honduras, where the poverty was striking. There was little doubt that the people we came to serve had little, materially. Yet they seemed to have a spiritual wealth far greater than ours. They lived with dependency, surrender and joy unfamiliar to some of us despite our material wellbeing. The people who had little knew they needed to rely on God. They understood the secret Paul shares with us about contentment: "I can do everything through him [Jesus] who gives me strength" (Philippians 4:13).

Instead of focusing on what we don't have, we need a shift in perspective. Focusing on what we *do* have helps us live in a place of gratitude, thankful for the many blessings God has lavished on us.

Those of us on that mission trip seemed worlds apart from the Hondurans. We had food, shelter and our basic needs met. Yet those with little had a measure of joy that eluded most of us who lived a more comfortable life. Gratitude begets joy.

There are times when I'm hurting and I forget to express thanks, even though it is my biblical mandate: "Give thanks in all circumstances, for this is God's will for you in Christ Jesus" (1 Thessalonians 5:18). Notice the little word "all" in this verse. We are to give thanks in *all* things—not *some* things or just the things that make us happy or are fun. Whether the troubles are hurled at us at 90 miles an hour (like a death) or slowly lobbed in our direction (like a string of insignificant annoyances), gratitude can disappear in a hurry. Yet it is precisely in these times that God will reveal Himself to you in new and tender ways if you turn to Him in gratitude rather than away from Him in contempt.

God will help carry both you and your burdens through the flooded valleys when life throws you troubles, and He will place you down gently when the ground becomes smooth again. Gratitude propels us forward. God is there with you every step of the way.

Lightening the Mother Load: Gratitude is the attitude God yearns to cultivate in us in all circumstances.

Musings for Moms:
- Think about a lean time in your life. How difficult was it to experience and express gratitude? How can you encourage your children to be thankful, no matter what?

- Philippians 4:5 says, "Let your gentleness be evident to all." Do you think of yourself as gentle? Would your children use the word "gentle" to describe you? How does gentleness relate to gratitude?

- According to Philippians 4:6, what is the remedy for anxiety? How often do you remember to utilize it?

Give It Your Best Shot

Snapshot from Henrietta: Colossians was a letter by Paul, written to correct heresies that had crept into the church at Colosse, located about 100 miles east of Ephesus and planted by a convert of Paul's named Epaphras. Epaphras needed help in order to help his misguided sheep, and he knew right where to go. Paul served as the chief shepherd trainer. He had the gift of communication, and now he put it to use to correct some wrong beliefs that had sprung up, which included a mixture of Greek, Oriental and Jewish religions.

Mom Moments with Miss Mears

Her Synopsis:
Colossians Portrays Jesus Christ, Our Life

Her Suggested Bible Readings:
Colossians 1:10-14   Praise and thanksgiving
Colossians 2:6-7,13-14 Living in Christ
Colossians 3:1-2,13-14 Holy living

Momento: No matter what you do, give it 100 percent.

Scripture: "Whatever you do, work at it with all your heart, as working for the Lord, not for men" (Colossians 3:23).

MAMA MIA

Each one of us has been entrusted with the gospel. We are commanded to share it with everyone to the ends of the earth. That's what missionaries do. And moms are missionaries too! The good news for moms is they don't have to travel any further than their home to reach their mission field.

One of the most challenging parts of my day starts at three o'clock when phase 2 starts. Each afternoon is complete with homework, taxiing, refereeing and cooking. (I am still challenged with fourth-grade homework. You would think by now I would know how to do fourth-grade math; after all, it's my fifth go-round—once for me, once for each of my kids.)

We walk through the laundry-room door and take up our usual posts. The girls perch at the kitchen table and empty their backpacks while I head to the coffeepot for fortification.

"Mom, I need you to sign these," Tianna said and handed me her folder.

"Mom, can you help me with my cursive?" moaned Nicole. "I hate doing cursive, plus I have to put all my spelling words in alphabetical order and there are like eight words that start with 'ae' . . ." Her voice trailed off in despair.

Cursive words three times each plus spelling in alphabetical order; it promised to be a long afternoon. I picked up Tianna's folder and took her papers out to sign them. One *C*, three *B*s and an *A*.

"Hey, Tianna, what happened here?" I asked, pointing to the *C*.

"Oh, that was social studies. It was so hard," she answered. But a little more digging revealed that she had spent more time socializing over the weekend than she had studying.

Then I turned my attention back to Nicole, whose handwriting was getting sloppier by the line. It was time to have a chat with both girls. The quality standard of giving their best had taken a nosedive.

"Hey, girls, listen up," I started, wanting to make sure I was encouraging, not lecturing. "How does it feel when you don't do as well at something as you know you can?"

"Well, I don't like it when our softball team doesn't play as well as they can," Tianna suggested tentatively.

"Exactly," I agreed. "Isn't it the same with your schoolwork? Don't you want to do the best that you can? Aren't you a little disappointed when you know you could have done better and you didn't quite give it your best shot? I know I am. I'm not really satisfied with myself if I know I haven't given something 100-percent effort. I may not always win or get great feedback, but as long as I give it my best shot . . . that's what matters." I wanted them to understand that the effort, not the result, was the key factor. We are to work at everything as if we were doing it for God.

"So," I continued, "listen to what the Bible says: 'Whatever you do, work at it with all your heart, as working for the Lord, not for men' [Colossians 3:23]. That means it's really between you and God, not you and me or your teacher or your coach." I paused and then added, "I know I like to make God smile, and I know that that's what you want too."

My message seemed to be registering. While I was talking, Nicole pulled out her eraser and rewrote some of her cursive, and Tianna got out her social studies book and reviewed her mistakes. I knew it was a lesson I needed to keep learning myself and keep reinforcing with my girls, but it was a start.

And I'm sure God was smiling.

Lightening the Mother Load: Pleasing God and giving things your best shot are winning life philosophies.

Musings for Moms:
· Does the amount of effort you put into a project depend on who you are doing it for? Is it as important to please your boss as it is to please God?

· Is your work as a mom recognized and rewarded as much as your roles outside the home? In what way is your work as a mom rewarded?

· Do you believe it is more important to reward your kids for effort or success?

Don't Believe Everything You Hear

Snapshot from Henrietta: Paul next shifted his attention to the church in Thessalonica. Despite the fact that there were enthusiastic believers in this church, their spiritual eyesight was a bit less than 20/20, especially when it came to recognizing the second coming of Christ. They had some confused and misguided notions regarding the return of Christ, which Paul needed to correct. He did so through this epistle of encouragement about Christian living.

Mom Moments with Miss Mears

Her Synopsis:
First Thessalonians Portrays Jesus Christ, the Coming One

Her Suggested Bible Readings:
1 Thessalonians 2:4,10-13   Encouragement for Holy living
1 Thessalonians 4:1-2   Living to please God
1 Thessalonians 5:11,14-18   Encouraging others

Momento: Don't believe everything you hear, and share only the truth. This lesson is important for moms and kids. Don't ever hesitate to use your experiences, even (or perhaps especially) the tough ones, to encourage others.

Scripture: "Therefore encourage one another and build each other up, just as in fact you are doing" (1 Thessalonians 5:11).

MAMA MIA

Too often we fall prey to believing everything we hear, and when the news is not the best, it can often be embellished. But how often do we stop to listen and find a way to encourage those who may be involved in the bad-news parent trap?

Women in particular enjoy talking, and kids are often one of our pet topics. But sometimes the stories we hear are not true but only half-truths and rumors. As moms, we can honor God by making sure we don't become part of the rumor mill by adding or repeating things we don't know to be true and, more so, by encouraging others who may be dragged down by such tales. I'm sure you can relate to the following story.

At first I didn't hear my neighbor Carly calling my name. I was just leaving the grocery store from an impromptu run and was too busy trying to guide my shopping cart down the curb without losing it.

"Kathy, how are you?" Carly's voice caught my attention. "I need to talk to you sometime. Jim told me I should talk to you—that you would understand and might be able to give me some advice." (Jim was the police chief in our town, so the sentence spoke volumes.) "I'm sure you heard about Max?" she paused, waiting for my reaction.

I hesitated, reluctant to repeat what I had heard, since I didn't know if it was true. "Well, I did hear something about tires or hubcaps, but I can't really remember what it was now," I answered truthfully. I had heard something briefly about her son, but surprisingly the rumor mill had been uncharacteristically quiet.

"Oh, good. I'm glad," she answered, clearly relieved.

"No, really, I didn't hear too much," I repeated, trying to reassure her.

Unfortunately, in our small town rumors typically thrive, taking on new life with each retelling. Instead of going to the source for the real story, people usually just believe and repeat what they hear. (Our family struggles have been the source of rumors more than once. I knew Carly was probably suffering from the same thing.)

My thoughts returned to the present conversation and how I could encourage her. "Absolutely, I would love to talk sometime!" I said without hesitation.

"I hope you don't mind that Jim said I should talk to you; he didn't think you would," Carly continued tentatively. "He thought maybe you could give me some encouragement . . ."

"No, not at all. I wish there had been someone for me to talk to when we were going through a tough time," I added sincerely. "Call me. We can go for a cup of coffee, and you can tell me what's going on," I offered.

A look of appreciation washed over her face, not only for my willingness to share, but also for my desire to hear what had happened from her rather than others. I was reminded of a valuable truth: If we are not part of the problem or part of the solution, we don't need to be part of the conversation—unless we are invited to participate in that conversation.

We have all been guilty of repeating stories without knowing if they are true, but it is not something God wants us to do. We need to focus on honoring God by only sharing what we know to be true in order to lift up or encourage others. And that includes correcting rumors, if it is in our power to do so.

Lightening the Mother Load: God celebrates truth. Be a messenger of His truth and grace with others. Don't participate in gossip sessions unless it is to set the record straight and share the blessing of encouragement.

Musings for Moms:

• Have you ever been the brunt of a rumor? How did it feel? Was there anyone who encouraged you?

• Have there been times you have been able to be an encourager to others rather than perpetuate rumors?

• Have you ever taken a stand for truth when you were engaged in a conversation you knew to be perpetuating an untruth? How hard do you think it would be to take a stand for truth? Are you willing to make a covenant to stand against a rumor the next time you hear one? Were you viewed as an encourager?

Too Much Idling Will Ruin Your Engine

Snapshot from Henrietta: It wasn't long before Paul needed to get his pen out a second time to write to the church at Thessalonica. This time, he needed to encourage them to stop being lazy and step up to action. Paul warns them about idleness: "We command you, brothers, to keep away from every brother who is idle and does not live according to the teaching you received from us" (2 Thessalonians 3:6). The predominant philosophy in Thessalonica was, "Well, since Jesus is going to return anyway, we are saved and exempt from working." Paul reminded them, "Yes, Jesus is going to come back, but there is much you can do to serve Him until that time."

Mom Moments with Miss Mears

Her Synopsis:
Second Thessalonians Portrays Jesus Christ, Our Returning Lord

Her Suggested Bible Readings:
2 Thessalonians 1:3-7	God is just
2 Thessalonians 2:13-14	Called and chosen by God
2 Thessalonians 3:6-11	Warning against idleness

Momento: Moms who are idle and are busybodies tend to have kids who become idle and are busybodies, too.

Scripture: "We hear that some among you are idle. They are not busy; they are busybodies" (2 Thessalonians 3:11).

MAMA MIA

Moms play an important role in shaping their children into responsible adults. Every step of the way, there are lessons we can impart to help our children not to be idle and not to be busybodies. As moms, we all want to nurture our children's ability to become productive citizens.

I found one place in particular that provided fertile ground for learning about both productivity and idleness: the country club pool. When my older sons had their first summer jobs at the club, they learned about working and saving money. At the same club, my daughters learned a thing or two about becoming idle busybodies.

"I can't wait to catch up with you at the pool this summer," my friend Karen said, waving to me from across the parking lot. It was late May and the summer splash season was just around the corner. Karen was one person I had enjoyed hanging out with at the pool and I would miss her.

"Oh, we let our membership lapse at the pool," I said with a sigh.

"Really?" she answered, surprised that I would give up our pool membership.

"Yeah, we're not around as much in the summer and it just isn't worth it for the time being," I answered, avoiding the other reason I didn't want to return: Too many maternal cliques had formed, and I didn't want my girls to fit in with the next generation of busybodies-in-training. There were various groups of moms who congregated at the pool, and I didn't feel particularly comfortable with any of them.

One group of moms allowed their girls to have carte blanche at the pool grill where they ate lunch every day. The food tab at the end of the summer rivaled the GNP of a small country. At times known for my frugality, unlimited lunches were off limits in my family, and my girls felt left out.

Another group of moms made it their business to monitor the status of guests and whether or not any contraband food had been brought in for snacks. I was reported more than once for serving illegal grapes to my girls rather than buying Nerds candy from the concession stand.

Then there was the group of moms who sat in the shade under a tree and caught up on the week's latest gossip while their kids took notes.

Sometimes I would join one of these groups, but more often I would take off for a lounge chair along the far end of the pool where I could be alone. I was quickly labeled as antisocial.

Predictably, the kids fell into their own little groups. One group of school-aged girls compared Vera Bradley bags. Another went off for tennis lessons in their coordinated outfits complete with matching hair scrunchies. Finally there were the bikini-clad tweens who sat at a picnic table, sipping their bottomless sodas while texting away on their cell phones. None of them were examples that I was completely comfortable having my girls emulate.

I became increasingly uncomfortable with the daily pool routine and decided it was time to take a break before we succumbed to the habits of idleness and entitlement.

It was time to settle down and do what was right (see 2 Thessalonians 3:12-13). God wanted us to be busy, not busybodies, so we relinquished the pool membership for the time being and pursued other activities. We kept active by hiking, taking trips together as a family, and splashing around in the creeks at the state parks instead of at the pool.

Being busy about God's business with your family trumps being busy about the business of other people. And God has plenty of healthy options available!

Lightening the Mother Load: God longs for us to be busy at work for His kingdom, not for earthly cliques.

Musings for Moms:
• What habits do you have that encourage idleness? What could you replace them with?

• What kinds of behaviors can you model as a mom to reduce the chances of your kids becoming busybodies?

• Are the recreational options you provide your children ones that promote idleness or busyness?

Spreading the (Wrong) Word

Snapshot from Henrietta: The next three books of the New Testament are referred to as the pastoral Epistles because they are letters written to other church leaders (two were to Timothy and one was to Titus) rather than to the churches themselves. In these letters, Paul gives the younger church leaders instructions on how to run a church. Timothy was one of Paul's own converts, and Paul referred to him as "my son whom I love, who is faithful in the Lord" (1 Corinthians 4:17). It was evident that Paul wasn't going to trust the growing churches to just anyone. This letter was written to Timothy while he was acting as the pastor of the church in Ephesus; but more than simply guidance for Timothy, the letter became a handbook for Christian leaders for centuries to come.

Mom Moments with Miss Mears

Her Synopsis:
First Timothy Portrays Jesus Christ, Our Teacher

Her Suggested Bible Readings:

1 Timothy 1:5-7	Love from a pure heart
1 Timothy 2:1-5	Instruction on worship
1 Timothy 3:11; 4:4	Worthy of respect from others and self
1 Timothy 6:6-10	Godliness and contentment

Momento: Money and stuff—these traps are all around us and try to lure in moms and kids alike.

Scripture: "For we brought nothing into the world, and we can take nothing out of it. But if we have food and clothing, we will be

content with that. People who want to get rich fall into tempta-
tion and a trap and into many foolish and harmful desires that
plunge men into ruin and destruction" (1 Timothy 6:7-8).

MAMA MIA

Simplify. Embrace life. Enhance relationships. Increase joy. God,
not stuff, increases our contentment.

Too often I get sucked into believing my happiness and worth
is directly proportional to the amount of stuff I own. For some
reason this seems to become particularly noticeable during the
Christmas holidays. Rather than celebrating Christ at Christmas,
I get sucked into materialistic mayhem. I know I am not alone in
this: It is something many of my friends and neighbors succumb
to also. Maybe you can relate.

Christmas was around the corner and my to-do list was getting longer rather than shorter. Despite feeling pulled in a thou-
sand different directions, I decided to take a break and join a
neighbor for a mom's morning out. I should have known it would
feed the desire for more—a desire that had been dormant but was
now about to re-emerge.

I made my way up the brick walkway and admired the decorations gracing the hand-carved oak door. The hostess ushered me
in and the foyer opened to an exquisitely decorated great room
with swags of fresh greens gracing each mantle. The tree, adorned
with white and silver ornaments, stood in the center of the room,
its top branches reaching the ceiling. Twinkling white lights provided the perfect finishing touch.

A fire crackled in the fireplace and several varieties of coffee
were set out in carafes in the kitchen. And there was no shortage of
food: fresh-baked muffins, cinnamon buns, cookies and all kinds
of chocolate concoctions had been placed on beautifully decorated
tables in three different rooms.

The hospitality and food were exquisite, and no expense had
been spared in dressing the house for holiday grandeur. I felt a
twinge of holiday envy set in. I hadn't yet decorated my house, and
when I did get to decorating my mantle, the greens wouldn't be fresh.

Then my mind became preoccupied with a friend who was struggling to pay her utility bills. The cost of my neighbor's decorations could have paid for gifts for my other friend's entire family. Their Christmas promised to be lean, and my frame of mind changed radically. I was no longer in the mood for the conversation that I was about to become a part of. I had been brought back to what really mattered, and my desire for a perfectly decorated home started to wane.

"Oh, Kathy, it's so nice to see you!" gushed one of my neighbors. "You're from New York, right? We were just there with a bus trip; we had a great time!"

I had thought about going on the same bus trip with my girls but decided to pass. A full day in New York complete with Broadway show, trip to the American Girl Doll Store and eating out was more expense than I could justify right before Christmas, especially when my friend couldn't pay her electric bill.

"Yeah, I grew up in the city," I answered.

"How come you didn't come?" one of the other women asked.

"Just too much right before Christmas," I said. "Anyway, I can drive into the city anytime."

"Oh, it was so beautiful, but I know what you mean about too much. Just the trip to the American Girl Store cost me over $500. And the cabs to get cross town added up too. I think we spent about $100 in cab fare."

My head was spinning from how much money my neighbor had spent. The cab fare alone would have kept my friend's power turned on for another three weeks. Yet I realized that I was just as guilty as they were of shopping till I dropped.

It was time for another attitude adjustment. Maybe I could encourage a simpler way of life, a reminder to my neighbors that we could still be consumers but share more with those who had less, and not pursue more and more stuff for ourselves.

I excused myself and thanked the hostess, and I decided to follow up with a written appeal to my neighbors to share from their abundance:

Dear Neighbors,

As we gathered together recently for coffee, I was again reminded of how blessed we are. There are several people who do not share the same privileges we do. We all come into the world the same way with nothing and will also leave with nothing.

Won't you please consider sharing with those less fortunate during this Christmas season? I have a friend who is struggling financially and I would like to help make Christmas brighter for her family.

Let me know if you would like to participate; I hope to hear from you.

God had reminded me that we are all God's children, that those who have more need to reach out to those with less, and that the pursuit of more stuff for ourselves will not yield happiness. It is not riches we need to pursue but the richness of a relationship with Christ.

Lightening the Mother Load: God yearns for us to share with others. All of us can take the simple step by starting where we are, one step and one gift at a time.

Musings for Moms:
- In what ways can "ruin and destruction" result from discontentment?

- How do you model sharing for your children?

- One way to incorporate sharing with others is to give away one item for every new item your child receives. How difficult would this be to incorporate?

Grandma's Faith Legacy

Snapshot from Henrietta: Second Timothy is the last letter the apostle Paul ever wrote. It was written to Timothy from Rome during Paul's final imprisonment sometime between AD 64 and 68. Paul was waiting to die, and he knew his time on earth was coming to a close. This short epistle is very personal. Despite being in prison and facing death, Paul continued to think of others, mentioning 23 people in this intimate correspondence to Timothy. One of my favorite verses in the Bible is from this epistle: "For God did not give us a spirit of timidity, but a spirit of power, of love and of self-discipline" (2 Timothy 1:7). In this letter, Paul entrusts the leadership of the church in Ephesus to Timothy and tells Timothy to guard the gospel.

Mom Moments with Miss Mears

Her Synopsis:
Second Timothy Portrays Jesus Christ, Our Example

Her Suggested Bible Readings:
2 Timothy 1:7	A spirit of boldness
2 Timothy 2:24	Be kind
2 Timothy 4:18	God will rescue and protect us

Momento: Grandmothers are often instrumental in passing on the legacy of faith.

Scripture: "I have been reminded of your sincere faith, which first lived in your grandmother Lois and in your mother Eunice and, I am persuaded, now lives in you also" (2 Timothy 1:5).

MAMA MIA

Dr. Mears noted, "Someone said, 'When you want to make a great person, start with his grandmother'" (p. 571). My great-grandmother was that person in my dad's life, and she passed her strong faith in God to both of us.

Grandma Knauf was a special lady. She loved us with the same tender love that she had for her Savior, Jesus, and she shared it every opportunity she had.

When I was a kid, she came to visit a couple times a year from upstate New York. I remember going to meet her at the Greyhound bus stop, and I could hardly wait to throw my arms around her in a big hug. I loved to sit with her and listen to her tell me about God. She held me close and read me stories about how much Jesus loved me. When I got too old to sit on her lap, she would sit beside me and tell me other Bible stories and all about my dad when he was younger. I will cherish those memories forever.

Our visits continued until her death when I was in college. She never stopped modeling her love for God, and even though Jesus didn't become central in my life until years later, she had planted the seeds of faith in me. She had also planted the seeds of faith within my dad, and just weeks before he died, he and I were able to share with each other our deep love for Jesus.

I am certain that my dad is in heaven with Grandma Knauf, and I know they will be there to greet me when it is my time to leave this earth.

The legacy of God's love had been nurtured and passed on to both of us by one special woman, just as Lois had done with her grandson Timothy. We moms—we future grandmas—have an obligation to pass on our gift of faith.

Lightening the Mother Load: Allow God to use you to pass the legacy of faith on to future generations.

Musings for Moms:

· Was there a family member who helped plant the seeds of faith in you? How did that person plant the seeds?

- How can you become a woman of faith to the future generations in your family?

- How can you plant seeds of faith in children in your church? In your community?

Can I Have a Mentor?

Snapshot from Henrietta: Titus was another one of Paul's converts, a Gentile with a great leadership track record. He had helped settle earlier differences in the church in Corinth, so Paul figured he was up to the task of being shipped south to the island of Crete. This letter is full of practical advice, similar to 1 Timothy. It especially focuses on how to keep new believers on the right track. The group on Crete needed a strong leader to make sure they stayed on course, because they were beginning to think that the gospel of grace needed the addition of legalism (rules) in order to be valid. Paul is careful to point out that we are not saved *by* good works but that we are saved *for* good works.

Mom Moments with Miss Mears

Her Synopsis:
Titus Portrays Jesus Christ, Our Pattern

Her Suggested Bible Readings:
Titus 2:3-4,11-12	Teaching older women
Titus 3:3-11	Doing what is good

Momento: The older generation is considered wiser for a reason.

Scripture: "Likewise, teach the older women to be reverent in the way they live, not to be slanderers or addicted to much wine, but to teach what is good" (Titus 2:3).

MAMA MIA

There's a popular saying that "it takes a village to raise a child." Sometimes, it takes a village of experienced moms to help us through the new and challenging experiences ahead. Sometimes, the mentors are our own moms, but there are times we need to broaden the circle of support.

One of those times for me was when I breastfed my first baby. Neither my mom nor my mother-in-law had breastfed, so I couldn't look to them for advice. In fact, my mother-in-law believed that bottle feeding was the natural way to feed a baby. But I was eager to embark on the next chapter of mothering: breastfeeding.

I wasn't too concerned. I mean, how hard could it be? God gave me breasts to feed my baby, so I had all the equipment I needed for successful nursing. Or so I thought. Little did I realize that breastfeeding needed just as much preparation as childbirth!

My first attempts at breastfeeding were awkward, at best. I fumbled with my hospital gown, positioned pillows under my arms for support and then tried to wake my sleeping baby. I stroked his cheek, unwrapped him, tickled his feet and even stuck my finger in his mouth—all to no avail. After several more attempts to get him to wake up, I rang the call bell for the nurse. It was obvious I needed help, and I began to think that this might not be such a "natural" process after all. Or at least not one that came naturally to me . . .

The nurse entered the room, helped me position my baby and as soon as I exposed my breast, asked in a stern voice, "Honey, where is your nursing bra?"

"Nursing bra?" I squeaked.

Exasperated, she repeated, "Yes, your nursing bra."

I remained silent and admitted I didn't have one.

"Well," she said, "you're going to need one."

I finally got the baby to latch on and didn't dare move. While the baby suckled away, my thoughts turned to getting a nursing bra. The only option I could think of was that my husband was going to need to shop for me.

A little bit later in the afternoon, Howie came to visit bearing gifts of chocolate, and I braced myself for what I needed to ask him.

"Howie," I began, tentatively, "the nurse says I need a nursing bra."

"That's nice," he answered, clearly not understanding the implications of my statement.

"Well, like while I'm in the hospital," I paused, waiting to see if the meaning of my statement had registered. It hadn't.

Before I could rephrase my question, the nurse re-appeared and sized up the situation with one glance.

"Has your wife told you she needs a nursing bra?"

He nodded his head affirmatively while the nurse and I worked together to get Chris to latch on to my other breast. But Howie obviously still did not understand what he was being asked to do.

The nurse finally said to Howie, "Well, you will need to go shopping."

He still didn't get it.

"Howie," I said hesitantly, "I guess one of the things they didn't tell us in class was that I needed a nursing bra."

He continued to look at me with a blank expression on his face.

I continued. "The nurse told me I need it now, so you are going to have to go buy one for me because it can't wait till I get home and I can't leave to do it myself." There. I managed to get the words out.

Howie continued to stare back at me, this time stating the obvious. "How will I know what size to get?" This was followed quickly by, "You're kidding, right?"

We muddled through as best we could, but we quickly learned that there had to be a better way. And that better way would have been to have had an experienced older woman as a mentor, someone who had walked ahead of me and who had breastfed. She no doubt would have pointed out—ahead of time—that I would need a nursing bra. Such a mentor could walk alongside me in the journey of parenting.

Anytime we embark upon something new, we need a teacher to help guide us. A mentor would have made a tremendous difference for me, but the good news is, it isn't too late for the next generation. Become a mentor to someone else. God will support you as you help someone along his or her way in life.

Lightening the Mother Load: God provides us with teachers and mentors who help us *grow through* rather than simply *go through* life's experiences.

Musings for Moms:

• Have you had a mentor in your life? How did that person make a difference?

• What gifts has God given you that you could or do use to mentor others?

• What are the differences between someone who provides support and someone who truly mentors?

Welcome Back

Snapshot from Henrietta: Dr. Mears refers to the book of Philemon as "a book in applied Christianity, a textbook of social service" (p. 584). Talk about divine appointments! Paul met Onesimus, a runaway slave, and shared the gospel with him, leading yet someone else to believe in Christ. But the story doesn't end there. In another divinely arranged detail, it turns out that Paul knew Onesimus's master, the one he stole and ran away from, a guy named Philemon. Paul knew Philemon from his church-planting days in Colosse, where Philemon was a fellow believer. So what did Paul do? He appealed to Philemon as a friend and brother in Christ and asked him to forgive Onesimus. Paul also assumed personal responsibility for Onesimus's debt, thereby in effect canceling it. Paul took on the sinner's debt, just like Christ did for us.

Mom Moments with Miss Mears

Her Synopsis:
Philemon Portrays Jesus Christ, Our Lord and Master

Her Suggested Bible Readings:
Philemon 4-7   Thanksgiving and prayer
Philemon 8-25   Paul's plea

Momento: Being welcoming is a practice that we need to instill in our kids.

Scripture: "So if you consider me a partner, welcome him as you would welcome me" (Philemon 17).

MAMA MIA

Welcoming and extending a hand of hospitality to others is a valuable gift we can share with other women and a skill we need to practice and impart to our children. The hurt that can result if it is withdrawn should not be underestimated.

I remember the deep pain I felt one time when an invitation to an event I looked forward to attending had—at least for a time—been rescinded.

I dialed Heather's number and hoped I would reach her. The cookie exchange was only two days away and I didn't want to mess up her plans for Sunday afternoon, but I knew there was no way I could bake four dozen cookies between now and then.

I was looking forward to spending time with a group of friends; I needed their company and support now more than ever. We were going through a difficult period with our younger son, Matt, and Nicole was still a nursing infant, which made juggling family responsibilities a challenge.

"Hello?" I heard Heather's voice on the other end of the receiver.

"Oh, Heather, I'm so glad you're home. Hey, listen, is it okay if I bow out of the cookie exchange on Sunday and just hang out with all of you? That won't be a problem, will it?" I went on to explain that we needed to go away for a family counseling weekend with Matt and that we wouldn't be back until right before the cookie exchange.

The long pause told me it would be a problem. "Well, actually, yes, it is a problem," Heather said, her voice now stiff and distant. "It wouldn't be fair to everyone else if you didn't bring cookies."

Perhaps she had misunderstood. I wanted to hang out with my friends. I just didn't want to participate in the exchange. "Oh, but I don't need to take any cookies home with me," I said, trying to clear up any misunderstanding. "I just want to come and enjoy everyone's company."

But she had not misunderstood. It wasn't okay. "No, Kathy," Heather said, her voice reflecting her obvious irritation. "It wouldn't be fair. I don't think you should come."

I was hurt and dismayed by her words. Heather had been one of my closest friends and a huge help after Nicole had been born. She had brought meals and extended gracious hospitality, which now seemed to be a forgotten memory.

Finally, she responded by offering to make my cookies for me.

"I'm not asking you to do that. Can't I just come and forget the cookies? Or stop at the store and pick some up?" I asked, really not understanding why homemade cookies were such a big deal.

"No, I'll make the cookies for you," she insisted and then asked for more details about Matt.

Now it was my turn to remain silent. The conversation had gone from cookies to an impersonal inquiry about my toughest experience to date as a parent. Shortly thereafter, the awkward conversation ended. I had gone from being a welcome part of the group to feeling like an outsider, all within just a few minutes.

After I hung up the phone, I no longer felt that I would be welcome at the event. I felt as if I had committed a wrong in wanting camaraderie but not cookies. I wondered, *Where was a playing out of the Christian mandate Paul so eloquently addressed in the book of Philemon?* The welcoming hand of hospitality should be extended to everyone and should never be withdrawn. Ambassadors for Christ are not to stand in judgment.

Lightening the Mother Load: Welcoming other Christians as brothers and sisters is a mandate from God; rely on grace and forgiveness to pave the way in difficult or awkward situations.

Musings for Moms:

• Are you careful to be as courteous and tactful as Paul was to Philemon in your dealings with others?

• Have you ever extended an invitation and wished you hadn't? What did you do about it?

• How do you feel about welcoming someone into your group of friends who is different from you?

Discipline and Disciple

Snapshot from Henrietta: The book of Hebrews is a book of encouragement (possibly written by Paul) to the first-century Jewish Christians who were about to engage in a huge pity party. Not that they didn't have good reason to have a pity bash: They were being persecuted, but this time—unlike in Moses' day—the persecution didn't come from foreign oppressors but from their own people. Their new faith wasn't mature enough yet to be able to keep them from thinking about chucking it altogether. They needed encouragement big time to hang in there with their new faith. They were beginning to feel as if "they had lost everything—altar, priests, sacrifices—by accepting Christ" (p. 592). They needed to be reminded of what they had in their belief. Dr. Mears writes, "Hebrews shows skill in dealing with the discouraged Jewish believers in Jesus. The writer tells all that we have in Christ. . . . This book was written to strengthen the faith of wavering believers. Paul's great argument is the superiority of Christ over all others" (pp. 592-93).

Mom Moments with Miss Mears

Her Synopsis:
Hebrews Portrays Jesus Christ, Our Intercessor at the Throne

Her Suggested Bible Readings:

Hebrews 1:14	Angels
Hebrews 10:19-25	Perseverance
Hebrews 12	God's discipline
Hebrews 13	Knowing love

Momento: To discipline is to teach, not to punish.

Scripture: "And you have forgotten that word of encouragement that addresses you as sons: 'My son, do not make light of the Lord's discipline, and do not lose heart when he rebukes you, because the Lord disciplines those he loves, and he punishes everyone he accepts as a son'" (Hebrews 12:5-6).

MAMA MIA

Because we are God's children, He disciplines us and sets boundaries for healthy living. As parents, it is our job to do the same with our kids. I am thankful God is my teacher!

While discipline might feel like punishment, it is really teaching about living within the confines of God's timeless truths. And the Bible is there to give us lots of practical advice when it comes to making followers (disciples) out of our kids.

Go back to the book of Proverbs and you will find lots of advice; the book really is a primer for parents. No need to scour the parenting books at your local bookstore. Simply pick up your Bible for some handy pointers. Here are a couple of pointers I have gleaned from God's Word that encourage me as I continue along the road of motherhood:

- Discipline out of love. Proverbs 13:24 says, "He who loves him is careful to discipline him."

- Hating discipline and spurning correction lead to ruin and won't make you popular, but then again parenting isn't a popularity contest. "You will say, 'How I hated discipline! How my heart spurned correction! I would not obey my teachers or listen to my instructors. I have come to the brink of utter ruin'" (Proverbs 5:12-14).

- Those whom the Lord disciplines are called blessed. "Blessed is the man you discipline, O LORD, the man you teach from your law" (Psalm 94:12).

Instead of simply telling your child that you are disciplining him or her for his or her own good, explain to the child why discipline is necessary: There are consequences for breaking rules. You are teaching your child how to follow the natural rules of life.

My kids have given me lots of practice in this regard (and I have given God lots of practice too!). The old adage "Little kids, little problems—big kids, big problems" holds true.

Natural consequences are a great mode of discipline and seem to help us all become disciples.

"If you don't wear socks, your feet might get cold."

"If you forget your homework folder at school, you will have to stay in at recess to finish it."

"If you don't return your sister's sweater, she may never let you borrow her clothes again."

"If you cheat on a test, you may get a zero."

"If you drive over the speed limit, you may get a ticket."

"If you smoke pot, you may get arrested."

"If you break the rules, you may go to jail."

The hard part for parents is to stand back and allow their kids to experience the outcomes of their poor choices without swooping in for the rescue. Becoming and developing effective disciples always includes discipline. Wrong choices and consequences will mold behavior. As God's children, we are accustomed to that message and grow closer to Him through it!

Lightening the Mother Load: God allows us to make choices and suffer the consequences of poor decisions; we must allow our kids that same opportunity.

Musings for Moms:
• When has God disciplined you? What happened, and how did you feel?

• What can happen when it is anger that prompts discipline? Have you ever disciplined out of anger?

• What is or has been your most difficult discipline challenge?

Pure Pain Is Pure Joy

Snapshot from Henrietta: The book of James is where the rubber meets the road in Christian living. It is an instruction manual of how to be a Christian. Believed to be written by James, Christ's brother, it is "the most practical of all the Epistles, and has been called 'A Practical Guide to Christian Life and Conduct.' This book is the Proverbs of the New Testament" (pp. 603-604). James didn't actually profess faith in Christ until after Jesus died on the cross, but he eventually became a leader in the Early Church. He talks a lot about pain and suffering (something he knew a thing or two about), and a key part of his message is how to walk the talk, emphasizing the importance of doing so. James believed that people ought to be able to tell a person is a Christian simply by how that person lives his or her life.

Mom Moments with Miss Mears

Her Synopsis:
James Portrays Jesus Christ, Our Pattern

Her Suggested Bible Readings:
James 1:1-12   Perseverance
James 2:12-26   Faith without works is dead
James 3:1-6   Taming the tongue

Momento: Maternal love, like God's love, is a love that simply never gives up.

Scripture: "Consider it pure joy, my brothers, whenever you face trials of many kinds, because you know that the testing of your faith develops perseverance" (James 1:2-3).

MAMA MIA

One of the most beautiful qualities of God's love for us is that it never, ever gives up. No matter what we may say or do, God will never stop loving us or pursuing us to join or return to His family. It is a love that is so vast it is almost incomprehensible. The closest I can come to understanding the depth of God's love for me is through the lens of a mother's love. A mother's love also never gives up.

Unfortunately, a maternal requirement to hang in for the long haul, no matter what, doesn't always come naturally. There are days that instead of forging forward, I feel more like crawling into a hole. Have you ever felt that way?

I know that trials help hone our perseverance (if we don't give in to impatience). After all, as Dr. Mears reminds us, "God makes our trials the instrument of blessing" (p. 606); and James reminds us that it is "the testing of your faith [that] develops perseverance" (James 1:3).

Dr. Mears acknowledges, though, that the problem is impatience: "Too often our trials work impatience, but God will give grace that His real purpose may be accomplished. Patience is more necessary than anything else in our faith life" (p. 606).

It is often journeying through life's greatest pains that yield the greatest joy when we emerge from the experience. But without perseverance we wouldn't make it through.

The pain of childbirth quickly fades when our heart is captivated by our newborn baby, innocent and momentarily immune to the challenges of life ahead. There are many times I wish I could take our child's place when he or she goes through a painful or difficult experience. How I wish I could give my arm for a routine immunization, stand up to the class bully, take on the hurt from the rejection of a first crush or the disappointment of not being selected to the All-Star team.

I will pursue my kids through their peaks and valleys with a love that never gives up, and I will be blessed because of it. "Blessed is the man who perseveres under trial, because when he has stood the test, he will receive the crown of life that God has promised to those who love him" (James 1:12). I take my encouragement from God, who is both desperate and determined to have a relationship with all of us. His desire is that none shall perish (see 2 Peter 3:9), and He pursues us relentlessly. His love keeps me going.

One of the deepest valleys I walked through was that of substance abuse. It required perseverance and determination I wasn't sure I had. As it turned out, I didn't, but God did.

God's love fueled my determination. I was determined to see my marriage survive. I was determined to fight for Matt's life. I was determined to have a relationship with my son. I was determined not to drown in the sea of despair. I was determined that Matt would finish high school and go on to college. I was determined to cling to the promise that God had a plan and would travel this journey with me.

God did, and my faith was strengthened because of it. Now I am on the other side, and the blessings are much easier to see in hindsight. Yet without perseverance, I would have missed the view.

Never give up; God doesn't.

Lightening the Mother Load: God never gives up on us. Likewise we must never give up on our children.

Musings for Moms:
- Think of a time when you felt like giving up but didn't. What did this experience teach you?

- Read Romans 5:3-5. Do you think perseverance always accompanies suffering?

- When you need to take a break to refuel, what do you do?

A Mission of Submission

Snapshot from Henrietta: Peter. Remember Peter? He was the one who denied Christ three times before Jesus was led to His crucifixion. Well, here he is writing to the first-century Christians, who are scattered hither and yon, to encourage them and also to warn them about the very real dangers of Satan. Satan, he notes, is always prowling around looking for someone to devour, and who better to prey on than a preoccupied, distracted new believer?

Peter communicates his message through his personal testimony, a powerful tool we still have at our disposal today. There is something very moving about hearing someone's story of personal transformation through Jesus.

Mom Moments with Miss Mears

Her Synopsis:
First Peter Portrays Jesus Christ, Precious Cornerstone of Our Faith

Her Suggested Bible Readings:
1 Peter 1:13-15	Be holy
1 Peter 3:1-22	Meek and quiet spirit
1 Peter 5:6-11	Humility and strength

Momento: Generously share with others whatever gifts or talents you have.

Scripture: "Each one should use whatever gift he has received to serve others, faithfully administering God's grace in its various forms. . . . If anyone serves, he should do it with the strength God provides, so that in all things God may be praised through Jesus

Christ. To him be the glory and the power for ever and ever. Amen"
(1 Peter 4:10-11).

MAMA MIA

God is a generous giver; He gives freely, not out of obligation, but out
of love. In fact, we have been given "every spiritual blessing in Christ"
(Ephesians 1:3). Yet God doesn't want us to hoard the gifts He has
given us, which include our talents, gifts, skills and abilities; rather,
He wants us to share them with others. There is no one else that has
the unique combination of gifts as you do, so you are uniquely
equipped to serve as His agent to accomplish His work here on earth.

It's exciting and not difficult or costly to participate on God's
team of abundant blessings. As a mom, you have several opportunities to share your gifts with others.

- Offer to watch your friend's older kids for an afternoon,
  so that she can have some valuable time alone with her
  new baby.
- The next time you cook a meal, double the recipe and
  bless someone with a hot meal when he or she least ex-
  pects it.
- Are you crafty? Do you knit? Rubber stamp? Why not
  surprise someone with a homemade gift?
- Everyone enjoys receiving a card. Why not take the time
  to write a just-thinking-of-you card to several women
  over the next month?
- The gift of time is invaluable to those who live alone.
  Visit someone who lives alone, and listen to whatever the
  person has to tell. Or offer to help do yard work or run
  an errand.

Many of these blessings can be shared with your children also;
include them in the practice of reaching out and sharing with others, not just those you already know, but new friends as well. What
a great way to introduce others to God's love. Give out of God's
overflowing love for you.

Lightening the Mother Load: Don't limit your gifts to financial generosity. Gifts of your time and talents are a beautiful way to share the gift of yourself with others.

Musings for Moms:
· What is the most thoughtful gift you have ever received?

· What gift have you received that has given you the most joy? Can you describe a gift that you gave someone else that brought you immeasurable joy?

· What factors make a gift great?

Hurry Up and Wait

Snapshot from Henrietta: In his first letter, Peter encouraged the new believers and warned them about evils from outside the church. In this second letter, Peter warns them about a different source of evil; one that came from inside the church. It appears that gossiping and correction in the name of Christ was as alive and well in the first century as they are today. New believers needed to be warned that there were some within their ranks who were not so kind or who were prone to not speak the truth in love. Peter cared deeply that his fellow believers hang in there, addressing them in endearing terms. But he doesn't waste any time referring to the slip-sliding backsliders as anything but what they were: "sows" and "dogs" (2 Peter 2:22). He also notes that those who once believed but have fallen away in their faith are worse off than those who never believed in the first place (see 2 Peter 2:21).

Mom Moments with Miss Mears

Her Synopsis:
Second Peter Portrays Jesus Christ, Our Strength

Her Suggested Bible Readings:
2 Peter 1:3-11	Faith and goodness
2 Peter 2:15-22	Falling off course
2 Peter 3:1-18	Christ our hope

Momento: Mothering is full of "hurry up and wait" scenarios. Think of them as manifestations of love.

Scripture: "The Lord is not slow in keeping his promise, as some understand slowness. He is patient with you, not wanting anyone to perish, but everyone to come to repentance" (2 Peter: 3:9).

MAMA MIA

God is a patient parent, and we need to turn to Him for guidance in this department.

Dr. Mears noted that "patience is more necessary than anything in our faith life" (p. 606), and we get practice in this department with our kids sometimes even as early as conception.

Was God's timing out of sync with your timing of when you wanted to conceive?

Did your baby stay comfortably (for him or her, not you) inside your uterus two weeks beyond your due date?

Did your toddler learn and practice the word "no" weeks before another word was added to the toddler's working vocabulary?

Does your daughter spend a disproportionate amount of time in the bathroom or on the phone?

Does your teenager consistently push the curfew to the eleventh hour?

How about term papers? Do they get written the night before they are due?

Our kids will give us lots of practice in ripening the fruit of our patience. And I will let you in on a secret: I am not the most patient person in the world. Are you? Maybe your life is like mine, guaranteed to sprout unexpected events and interruptions when my patience is wearing thin. God obviously understands that I need more practice at this skill—so He keeps giving me more practice! A recent roller-skating party with Nicole gave me my last practice session.

We arrived late and then spent the next 57 minutes getting her skates on. And I managed not to lose my patience, temper or sanity in the process.

"Mom, can I get Rollerblades?" Nicole asked, knowing that she could skate faster with in-line skates.

"Sure, why not?" I answered, eager to get her skates on, so she could join the fun.

"They don't feel right," she answered in predictable fashion. (Even the seams on her socks bother her if they are not lined up perfectly, something I still cannot help her with after 10 years.)

The Rollerblades they had at this skating rink were adjustable, but we couldn't get them to adjust to her feet.

"I want to try the other kind," she finally decided after several unsuccessful attempts at getting the Rollerblades to fit.

So we went back up to the counter and traded the Rollerblades in for tan ankle-boot skates with large red wheels.

"Mom," she moaned, throwing her head back and glaring at the ceiling, "the tongue feels funny and the lining has a bump in it."

We must have taken them off and put them on 23 times. Finally when the tongue and lining were in place, it was time to lace them up.

"That's too tight. . . . No, now it's too loose. . . . This one is tighter than the other one. . . . Never mind, let me do it," she finally said.

"Gladly," I answered, sliding over on the bench.

Finally, an hour after we arrived, she went out to skate. The session was half over, yet I had never raised my voice, sighed or rolled my eyes. God knew I would need an extra dose of patience that day, and He very generously gave me that extra portion.

I'm sure there are days when you need an extra portion (or two) of patience. God is a gracious giver and will be delighted to honor your request when you seek His help.

Lightening the Mother Load: Patience is one of the fruits of the Spirit (see Galatians 5:22-23). Make sure it is ripe and succulent.

Musings for Moms:

• Do you think of patience more as a manifestation of love or as allowing yourself to be manipulated?

• Read Galatians 5:22-23. Where does patience rank for you among the fruits of the Spirit in your life? What factors influence your ability to demonstrate patience?

• What blessings might you experience if you increased your ability to be patient?

A Lesson in Sharing

Snapshot from Henrietta: First John, a short epistle, was written by Jesus' beloved disciple, John, in his golden years. He writes to all Christians, young and old, to encourage and assure them of their salvation and eternal life with Christ. His words are sensitive and compassionate yet firm in telling Christians that they must not only believe like a Christian, but also live like a Christian. It's that walk-the-talk message again. With right behavior and right belief come right rewards.

Mom Moments with Miss Mears

Her Synopsis:
First John Portrays Jesus Christ, Our Life

Her Suggested Bible Readings:

1 John 2:15-17	Don't love the world
1 John 3:1-24	Children of God
1 John 4:7-12	God's love

Momento: There is great beauty in sharing.

Scripture: "If anyone has material possessions and sees his brother in need but has no pity on him, how can the love of God be in him?" (1 John 3:17).

MAMA MIA

"John says we not only must believe like Christians, but we also must act like Christians" (pp. 640-641). One of the most tangible and visible ways we can demonstrate the love of Christ in us is by living our faith on a daily basis, finding ways to share what we have with others.

My garage ministry, as I affectionately referred to it, was booming. One day, a neighbor stopped by with five large bags full of gorgeous children's clothes. "Kathy, are you still taking donations in your garage?" she asked. "I'd like to leave these things here with you if you're still accepting donations for people who could use kids' clothes." She gestured to the bags in her car.

"Wow, that's great!" I answered, delighted with her thoughtfulness. "I would love to go through them and distribute them to people who can use them. I know lots of families that will benefit from your generosity."

The clothes were beautiful: Gymboree, Gap and several other brand names, some with tags still on. The bags contained a gold mine of clothing. Boys and girls clothes of different sizes were all mixed together, so I sat down on the family-room floor, ready to sort them.

"Can I help, Mom?" Nicole asked.

"Sure," I answered, happy for the help.

We got to work separating the clothing by size. As Nicole went through some of the baby things, she found a little sleeper and asked if she could dress her baby doll in one.

"Sure, Nicole," I answered, thinking nothing of it.

We continued going through the clothes, putting baby boy things in one pile, toddler girls in another, bigger boys in yet another, and before too long our task was complete.

I made some calls and had families all picked out to receive the new clothes. I packed the bags in the back of my car, ready to distribute, beaming with delight. What a blessing this would be!

My joy, however, was short lived. The next day at the pool, the woman who had given me all the clothes approached me while I was swimming.

"Kathy, would you come here?" she said, her tone indicating she wasn't too happy.

"Sure," I answered.

She didn't waste any time getting to the point.

"Kathy," she addressed me abruptly. "I was changing the baby and I saw this outfit on Nicole's doll." She held out the outfit she had stripped off Nicole's doll in her left hand.

She continued to address me, her voice now tainted by the same anger that was visible in her face. "I didn't give you those things to end up on Nicole's baby doll. I didn't even let Jacob play with them . . .

they were very special to me. They weren't meant to be put on some baby doll."

I tried to explain what had happened, but my words fell on deaf ears. Her mind was made up. All my efforts at explaining what had been an honest mistake went unaccepted. I was sad and confused. What had been a gift was now being reclaimed.

"I'm sorry," I said, at a loss for words. "I've already called the families," I added, my voice trailing off.

But it didn't change her mind. She wanted all the clothes returned.

"I am going to give the clothes to Jen," she stated. "Her kids will wear them, not their dolls." Instead of the clothing going to families who couldn't afford them, they were being given to a neighbor who was an attorney and whose husband was a physician! I was grieved, and so was Nicole.

"Why did she take back all those clothes, Mommy?" Nicole asked. "Didn't she want to share with other people?" she added.

"I guess not," I answered honestly.

"That's sad, Mommy," Nicole said.

And I agreed with her.

The example that had been set was one of selfishness, not sharing. And it wasn't an example that either God or I wanted to emulate.

Lightening the Mother Load: Discouragement is part of life. Don't allow Satan to thwart your plans to bless others or steal your joy. Continue in your efforts to bless others through sharing. God honors your efforts, even if they derail.

Musings for Moms:
· How difficult is it for you to live a life that matches your faith convictions?

· What can you do to incorporate more giving into your life?

· How can you teach sharing to your children?

Friends Don't Forsake

Snapshot from Henrietta: Second and 3 John are the shortest books in the New Testament, and 2 John is the only book in the Bible written to a woman. This gal evidently not only had wonderful hospitality skills but also had the propensity to be taken advantage of. There were plenty of false prophets who wanted to stop by for afternoon tea or a meal. John warns this generous woman not to get suckered in to feeding or entertaining them, because if she did, she would actually end up participating in their wicked ways. This warning is still useful advice today, as there are lots of people out there claiming to love God but really only looking to exploit the kindness of Christians.

Mom Moments with Miss Mears

Her Synopsis:
Second John Portrays Christ, the Truth

Her Suggested Bible Readings:
2 John 1-13   Walking in truth

Momento: Friends love each other through both good and bad times.

Scripture: "And now, dear lady, I am not writing you a new command but one we have had from the beginning. I ask that we love one another" (2 John 5).

MAMA MIA

Above all we are commanded to love one another. Sometimes to truly love each other moves us from a place of comfortable complacency to courageous compassion.

"Chara, how are you?" I asked, concerned about how weak her voice sounded.

"Oh, not so good," she answered honestly. "I've just gotten out of the hospital; this time I was there for almost three weeks."

"Three weeks?" In today's world of drive-through hospital stays, three weeks is virtually unheard of.

"Yeah, this time was rough, but I'm feeling a little bit stronger now." Then she paused. "I'd really love it if you could come to visit," she added, her voice wistful with the hope that I would visit and bring some memories of happier times with me.

Chara and I had known each other since third grade. This recent hospital stay was because she had been diagnosed with breast cancer. She valued and cherished her friendships deeply and nurtured them with love that always put the other person first. Now it was my turn to return that love.

"Yes, I'd love to come and visit," I answered without any hesitation. "Why don't I come for your birthday?" I asked. "We could have a special day together."

"Really? You would do that? Come all the way out here just for my birthday?"

Life had returned to her voice, and I knew that I would make the trans-continental trip a month later to spend her birthday with her. Any lingering doubts that I had were erased by the delight I had heard in her voice. "Absolutely!" I said. "I will call you back when I've booked my flight . . . I'm going to do that as soon as we get off the phone."

We chatted a bit longer, and when I got off the phone, I got to work planning my trip. I booked my flight and found a small bed-and-breakfast nestled in the foothills of the San Bernardino Mountains where we could spend her special day together—close, yet a world away. Satisfied with the details of my trip, I called her back.

"Already? You booked everything already? You're really coming? I am so excited I can hardly stand it!" she said all in one breathless sentence. And then she became silent.

"Chara, are you still there?" I was afraid we had been disconnected, but instead a very powerful connection had been forged.

"Kathy, I'm just so grateful you are coming. It will be so wonderful to see you."

I knew that this would be a special visit. I didn't know if it would be our last visit. I hoped not, but I did know that this visit was one motivated out of a decision to love, not passively, but actively.

John tells us, "I am not writing you a new command but one we have had from the beginning. I ask that we love one another" (2 John 5). He then goes on to prompt us to active love: "And this is love: that we walk in obedience to his commands. As you have heard from the beginning, his command is that you walk in love" (2 John 5-6). Such a display is not always easy, but it is what God both desires and demands of us. And He will give us the strength to move from complacency to compassion in loving others.

Lightening the Mother Load: Loving courageously may move you out of your comfort zone, but it will also yield incredible blessings.

Musings for Moms:
· What attributes do you value most in a friend?

· Think of a time you were able to share the gift of love with a friend. How did you feel?

· What are some of the ways you let your friends know that you value them?

Setting a Good Example

Snapshot from Henrietta: Third John has two main characters: Gaius and Diotrephes. Gaius was the good guy (remember G for "good"). He was the kind of guy who gives Christians a good name. He got it right, offering love and hospitality, especially to missionaries. He was wealthy and talented and shared everything he had with others. Remember, "hospitality is a manifestation of Christian love" (p. 652). Diatrophes, on the other hand, was not such a good guy. He was a troublemaker and a church official of the worst kind, constantly sticking his nose in Gaius's business (where it didn't belong) and trying to stir up trouble. Remember, "You can be either a Gaius, helping in the kingdom, or a Diotrephes, hindering the cause" (p. 652). I would much rather be a Gaius, wouldn't you?

Mom Moments with Miss Mears

Her Synopsis:
Jesus Christ, the Way

Her Suggested Bible Readings:
3 John 1-14   The Kingdom

Momento: Good examples are often the simplest acts or smallest gestures, yet often they carry the greatest impact.

Scripture: "Dear friend, do not imitate what is evil but what is good. Anyone who does what is good is from God. Anyone who does what is evil has not seen God" (3 John 11).

MAMA MIA

As moms we juggle lots of different responsibilities. Think back to the esteemed Proverbs 31 woman: mom, wife, businesswoman and model of hospitality and good stewardship. We have far more in common with her than we realize.

Many of us fulfill different roles, but doing what is good, even if it is something as small as a gesture of hospitality, is something all of us can do, regardless of our stage in life. While such a gesture may not always be convenient, it is always noticed.

Have you ever spontaneously invited someone in who shows up unannounced at your doorstep? Don't underestimate the impact a simple invitation into your home can have. Let me give you a personal example.

One day, the doorbell rang just as I was taking the second pot of burnt macaroni off the stove. (Unfortunately, this was nothing new; I have been known to put pasta on to boil, get distracted and forget about the pasta, and the next thing I know, I have another pot of burnt noodles.) I moved the burnt pasta, tripped over the cat and made my way to the front door.

My friend Karen was at the door. "Karen, how nice to see you. Come in, come in," I said, gesturing with the pasta spoon for her to follow me.

"Mom," Tianna called from the kitchen table where she, her sister and three friends were doing homework and patiently waiting for some edible food. "When is dinner going to be ready?"

My house was in a state of chaos, but that was nothing new.

"Oh, you're right in the middle of getting the kids food; I just came to drop off the book I borrowed," Karen said, somewhat embarrassed that she hadn't called before dropping by.

"Not at all. Do you have a minute? I haven't seen you in ages," I continued, still urging her to follow me with the pasta spoon. I decided hot dogs might be a better option than mac and cheese. "Just let me get these guys something to eat and if you have a minute we can catch up." I popped some hot dogs in the microwave and didn't budge. If anyone could ruin a hot dog, it would be me.

"Well, if you're sure," she said, the hesitation audible in her voice. "Nathan's still at basketball practice and I don't have to pick him up for 20 minutes."

"Absolutely," I answered, taking the hot dogs out of the microwave and putting them on the table with some ketchup.

"Okay, guys, here you go. I think there are popsicles for dessert too. You can help yourselves. I'm going to talk to Karen for a few minutes."

I wiped my hands on a soggy dish towel and flopped into one of the chairs in the other room. We caught up for a few minutes. It had been months since we had seen each other, so 20 minutes wasn't nearly enough time to catch up, but it was enough to cover the highlights.

Karen left, the kids finished dinner and their homework, and before I knew it, it was time for the girls' friends to go home. It had been a typical day.

Several months later I ran into Karen at the post office, and she brought up her impromptu visit to my house.

"Kathy," she said, "remember when I stopped by your house a few months ago to return that book?"

I nodded my head. How could I forget? It was one of those "Calgon, take me away" moments of my life.

"Well, I just want you to know how much it meant to me that you invited me in to visit for a few minutes when it was right in the middle of suppertime and you had other kids there and everything. It just didn't bother you at all. I would never be able to just invite someone in like that; I wish I could, but I can't. My house has to be perfect for me to have anyone over. I wish I could do what you did. That was true hospitality."

"Really?" I answered, somewhat surprised. What hadn't seemed like a big deal to me had obviously made a huge impression on her.

We chatted a bit more and I was reminded of a profound truth: One of the greatest acts of hospitality is the act of sharing oneself.

Relationships have and continue to be the most important thing to God. He yearns to engage you in a personal vibrant love relationship and also yearns for you to extend that love to others. Open yourself to being a conduit of God's love.

Lightening the Mother Load: People don't care how much you know until they know how much you care. People remember people who care.

Musings for Moms:
· When was the last time you offered someone your time?

· List three simple ways you can incorporate the gift of hospitality into your everyday life.

· How often do you practice hospitality without grumbling? How much time and effort do you believe is required to demonstrate hospitality? Does it have to be complicated?

Have Mercy and Keep the Faith!

Snapshot from Henrietta: Jude, Jesus' brother, wrote this epistle to address the dangers confronting the doctrines of the Early Church. There were people who denied the deity of Christ right inside the Church. There are *still* people like that right inside the Church! It was pretty tough being a believer in Christ as Messiah in the first century; if it wasn't the Jewish believers adding to the gospel, it was the Roman authorities bullying the early believers. Those who did hold fast to their beliefs really had their work cut out for them. Fortunately, they wrote their encouragement down, so it is still available for us today.

Mom Moments with Miss Mears

Her Synopsis:
Jesus Christ, Our Keeper

Her Suggested Bible Readings:
Jude 1-25   True saving grace

Momento: Share your faith gently; use words only when necessary.

Scripture: "But you, dear friends, build yourselves up in your most holy faith and pray in the Holy Spirit. . . . Be merciful to those who doubt" (Jude 20-22).

MAMA MIA

As moms, we hold a privileged place of influence for God in our lives. Every day in a variety of settings, both inside and outside of our homes, we have the opportunity to share our faith and influence others for God. But we need to heed the admonition to "be merciful to those who doubt" (Jude 22).

St. Francis noted that when we share the gospel, we should "use words if necessary." This is sage advice that allows us to share our faith quietly with those who may not yet believe. Actions speak loudly, and the quiet witness of a consistency between one's belief and one's life sends a powerful message. Strong words of rebuke are fine to share with those who do believe but have veered off the path of truth. But be merciful to those who doubt. I hate to admit it, but I flunked Faith Sharing 101.

When I first became a believer, I was excited! I made new discoveries about God every day. I learned about His promises and the power of the Holy Spirit. I was giddy with excitement! I was on fire for God. I was totally obnoxious!

"Hey, I've found the greatest thing since sliced bread. Do you want some?" I'd say to anyone who would listen.

"No," was the typical response.

"Oh, come on. Try some," I continued, my voice becoming slightly agitated.

Their answer was still the same: "No."

Yet it still didn't stop me from delivering my message. They were going to get what I had whether they liked it or not—or whether they wanted it or not. I was totally unfamiliar with the words from Jude. But over time, the same Holy Spirit I was so excited about intervened and led me to a gentler way of sharing my faith that had nothing to do with speaking words and everything to do with loving and serving others.

Occasionally, someone would ask why I gave or served in a certain way and that became my invitation to speak. "Why would you offer to come all the way over here to drive someone you have never met to a doctor's appointment?" "Why would you give my kids all these beautiful clothes when you could sell them at the consignment store?" "Why would you make such a generous donation to the fund-raising auction when you don't even know people in that organization?"

In these instances, I could share my motivation to serve Jesus out of my love for Him by loving and serving others. "Always be prepared to give an answer to everyone who asks you to give the reason for the hope that you have. But do this with gentleness and respect" (1 Peter 3:15). I was also reminded that it is not my job to win players to God's team. His Spirit would take care of that. My job was to demonstrate it was a team worth playing on.

So my methods changed, and I now consider my life my mission field. I don't shy away from sharing my faith, but I do realize that gentleness and sensitivity go a long way in making sure I am heard. I still have a long way to go but understand that if I am going to talk about the power of God's love, I must start by modeling it.

Your life can also be your mission field as you quietly and gently share your faith, introducing others to the most amazing relationship of their life.

Lightening the Mother Load: A quiet witness speaks the loudest even if (or perhaps especially when) words are absent.

Musings for Moms:
- Think about times when others have shared their faith with you. Which approach was the most effective? How can you incorporate that approach when you tell your own story?

- How do you share your faith? Are you pushy or merciful?

- Do you want to "snatch others from the fire" (Jude 23)? What silent acts can you do to accomplish this goal?

Birthing Pains:
The Joy of Life to Come

Snapshot from Henrietta: Revelation is a book of prophecy, the only such book in the New Testament. The visions were given to John while he was in exile on the Island of Patmos in the Aegean Sea. (Remember, John was Jesus' beloved disciple, who also penned his Gospel and 1, 2 and 3 John.)

The book is a glance at what we will experience when Christ returns, the close of the story of our redemption. Rather than being a doom-and-gloom projection of the end of the earth, it is a daring and glorious look ahead to the victory that Christ has over Satan in the final big-battle blowout. Take that, you slimy serpent! The ending has been written, and it features eternity with God—the God who created us, restored us and loves us.

Mom Moments with Miss Mears

Her Synopsis:
Revelation Portrays Jesus Christ, Our Triumphant King

Her Suggested Bible Readings:
Revelation 1:1-8   The Coming of Christ
Revelation 4:1-11   The Throne in Heaven
Revelation 19:1-10   Hallelujah!
Revelation 22:1-21   Christ the Lord of All

Momento: God's life is eternal; God's kingdom is here.

Scripture: "Behold, I am coming soon! My reward is with me, and I will give to everyone according to what he has done. I am the

Alpha and the Omega, the First and the Last, the Beginning and the End" (Revelation 22:12-13).

MAMA MIA

Revelation really isn't the last chapter, but rather the beginning. This final book of the Bible brings us full circle to redemption and everlasting life, the way life was originally designed and intended to be lived before the fall of man.

God promises us abundant life with Him, but in the meantime the kingdom of God is here. Each life, relationship and journey inevitably brings struggles, but along with those struggles is the promise of redemption through Jesus. It is that promise that sustains us.

As moms, we have many experiences (both positive and negative) that are woven into the tapestry of our lives. It is from both of these that we gain experience to carefully and lovingly teach our kids about the future. And what a glorious future the believers in Christ have! In the meantime, the immediate future of your children and of the Church is in your hands.

Lightening the Mother Load: Remember, you are not alone; God will never leave you or forsake you.

Musings for Moms:
- Do you believe that both the positive and negative parenting experiences provide beauty to the tapestry of your life as a mom?

- Does expectancy and hope for the life to come affect how you make decisions in the here and now in your family and with your children? How?

- What are some ways you can live a life that more fully represents the victory we have in Christ in our life on earth? How can you pass this along to your children?

As you contemplate the kingdom of God and serving Christ here on earth, I challenge you to embrace the following questions:

- How will you embark on the journey before you?

- What has God called you to do?

- How does God call you to respond to the needs you see around you?

- How can you fall more deeply in love with God and others on a daily basis?

- What does God want to teach you?

- How does Satan twist the same event to try to derail you?

- What can you do that will strengthen your relationship with God?

- How can good come from the devastation and hurt that come your way?

- How can the power of the Holy Spirit fuel you to live your life to the fullest in the present?

As you reflect on these thoughts and the experiences of other mothers, may you look to the pages of the Bible, God's parenting manual, to give you hope and encouragement. And may God bless you richly as you continue on your journey of motherhood.